Surrender the Joy Stealers:

Rediscover the Jesus Joy in You
Six-Week Bible Study

ENDORSEMENTS

Doris Swift's book, *Surrender the Joy Stealers*, provides Christian women with a wonderful promise of joy in Jesus—regardless of the momentary circumstances. The book provides a powerful study that targets the devastation of lost joy and assures the reader the solution is found in Christ. Power-packed with Scripture, the author also reminds the reader there's a balm for the broken heart: "Friend, God meets us in the thick darkness of our pain and calls us into his wonderful light." Don't miss this book!
—**Deb DeArmond**, writing coach and author of six books on marriage, family, and life after fifty.

We've all experienced times when life knocks us off our feet. Anxiety and fear set in, and joy seems like a distant memory. What I appreciate so much about Doris Swift's new Bible study, *Surrender the Joy Stealers: Rediscover the Jesus Joy in You,* is her realistic, solidly biblical, yet ultimately hopeful message. She doesn't ignore the awful realities of life, but urges us to rediscover God and His Word, to find truth that will help us navigate the tough days and experience joy even in the midst of suffering. Doris is someone who listens, cares, and communicates in such a down-to-earth way that you'll feel like you're opening the Bible with a good and caring friend. I highly recommend her Bible study to everyone who needs to rediscover their joy.
—**Jamie Janosz**, Managing Editor of Moody Bible Institute's *Today in the Word* devotional, and the author of *When Others Shuddered: Eight Women Who Refused to Give Up*.

Doris Swift has a heart for hurting women. She knows what it's like to struggle with our identity in Christ and to

accept his love. In *Surrender the Joy Stealers,* she guides women through a process of Bible study and prayer so that they might discover for themselves the abundant joy waiting for them through Christ. Though it's designed as a six-week study, there's enough material to stretch it out much longer. I can also see how repeating it could bring up new layers to experience and learn from. If you're going through a period of seeking but not finding joy, this is the study for you.
—**Sharon Wilharm**, host of *All God's Women* podcast and radio show and author of *Women of Prayer* Bible study

Surrender the Joy Stealers by Doris Swift is an easy-to-follow Bible Study but is deep and rich in the information we need to claim or reclaim our joy. As a joy girl myself, I appreciate how it focuses on identifying and overcoming the things that rob us of God's joy in our lives.

The study is rooted in biblical principles and uses Scripture in offering practical steps for surrendering these joy stealers to God. The study covers six principals: revealing joy, responding to it, receiving it, renewing mind and spirit, resting in God. and reaching out to others.

Surrender the Joy Stealers is designed for individuals or groups, but Doris, a Christian author and speaker who had led many Bible studies, strongly encourages readers to gather and study together for the most impact. I have known Doris for several years, and her sweet and kind demeanor leaps off these pages.

One feature I particularly liked is the useful Leader's Guide that takes you step-by-step in starting a Bible study group.

Surrender the Joy Stealers is a Bible study that offers valuable insights and practical guidance for anyone looking to find more joy in their life.
—**Yvette Walker**, founder of Positively Joy Ministries at positivelyjoy.com

Doris Swift shares personal stories, biblical guidance, and practical steps to help identify what steals our joy. *Surrender the Joy Stealers* engages us in a personal study to allow the transforming power of God's Word to reawaken the joy within us. Through this study, women will rediscover true joy in Jesus. This study will help many find joy.
—**Billie Jauss**, author of *Making Room* and *Distraction Detox*, podcast host of *The Family Room*, and national speaker.

There was a time when I believed the lie that I was "joy immune," while looking at others who seemed to overflow with joy as I crawled through depression's abyss. Through much time in prayer and in God's Word, it became clear that joy was a promise and a gift from God to his children, so as one of his children, I could not be joy immune. But I needed to address the joy stealers in my life. In *Surrender the Joy Stealers*, Doris helps her readers, through either individual or group Bible study, learn to identify the joy stealers in their life, surrender them to God, and receive the joy Jesus came to give. This is a timeless resource for those desiring to live in the fullness of joy Jesus offers!
—**Dr. Michelle Bengtson**, clinical neuropsychologist and award-winning author of *Hope Prevails*, *Breaking Anxiety's Grip*, and *Today is Going to be a Good Day*

Surrender the Joy Stealers: Rediscover the Jesus Joy in You is a biblically grounded study that offers hope and encouragement to readers struggling with life's challenges. Author Doris Swift speaks from her own experiences of heartache and struggle but also draws on timeless truths from the Bible. Her realistic yet ultimately hopeful message encourages readers to rediscover God and His Word and find joy despite suffering. Whether you've walked with the Lord for decades or just started your faith journey, this study will increase your faith and deepen your relationship with God.

—**Connie Albers**, host of the *Equipped to Be* podcast, media contributor, and author of *Parenting Beyond the Rules, Raising Teens with Confidence and Joy*

In *Surrender the Joy Stealers: Rediscover the Jesus Joy in You*, Doris Swift has written a truth-filled, relatable, and practical Bible study for all women who desire the abundant life Jesus offers. As stated in the introduction, "rediscover the joy Jesus gave you ... the overflowing, ever-present Jesus joy within." This is certainly what I want as I live out my calling! Focusing on Jesus's words recorded in John 15 is life-giving and transformational. Doris shares relatable personal stories to help women understand scriptural principles and walks us through the study of God's Word with insightful questions. Is there something ailing your soul today? Do you sense a general malaise among the women you encounter? Here's help! Gather a few friends, work through this study together, cooperate with God in the process, and discover the truth that "regardless of circumstances, we can still experience supernatural joy."

—**Jen Vogel**, National Director for Alliance Women 2015-2023

Surrender the Joy Stealers is not just a Bible study. Rather, it's an opportunity for transformation and knowing you're not alone. Doris Swift has masterfully integrated Scripture with psychological concepts giving us practical wisdom. While honoring our human journey, her stories illustrate deeper understandings.

You'll find hope and guidance throughout the six-week group study format. With clear guidelines for facilitators, this study will heighten your awareness. Especially valuable in

community, expect to grow your relationships and discover joy in Jesus along the way.
—**Judy K. Herman**, LPC-MHSP, speaker, psychotherapist, and author of *Beyond Messy Relationships: Divine Invitations to Your Authentic Self*.

Doris Swift has crafted a book that offers tremendous insight into growing closer to God and experiencing true joy in life. Through studying and applying Scripture, *Surrendering the Joy Stealers: Rediscover the Jesus Joy in YOU!* [emphasis added to title] helps readers find fulfillment in their daily lives, allowing them to deepen both their faith journey and relationship with our Lord. I highly recommend this essential guide for anyone looking to strive toward greater understanding of His word!
—**Misty Phillip**, founder of Spark Media, award-winning author of *The Struggle is Real: But So Is God* Bible study.

Over the past several years, sitting in the front-row seat and watching Doris live out the principles taught in *Surrender the Joy Stealers* has been a privilege. I am thrilled her lessons learned have found their way into this book. Through sound biblical teaching, dig-deeper questions, practical application, and relatable personal experiences, Doris leads us to live a joy-filled life, regardless of circumstances. Each turn of the page is an opportunity to gather tools, equipping us to fight for joy.
—**Evelyn Sherwood**, lover of Jesus, worship minister, blogger of *Hope for the Journey* at evelynsherwood.com

Scripture tells us that the joy of the Lord is our strength. But joy is not always readily found, especially when circumstances are grim. In *Surrender the Joy Stealers*, Ms. Swift offers a fresh, scriptural perspective that enables us to seek out and overcome the many things that can steal

our joy. Her excellent teaching and wisdom will be such a help to readers—worthy of both individual or group studies. This one is a winner!
—**Julie Zine Coleman**, author of *On Purpose: Understanding God's Freedom for Women through Scripture*, and managing editor of AriseDaily.com (the Advanced Writers and Speakers Association's devotional website)

In *Surrender the Joy Stealers*, Doris Swift helps us take a deep look at what's going on inside our hearts. Then based on God's truth, she leads us from hurt to healing and helps us to discover the deep, abiding joy that no circumstances can steal.
—**Tara L. Cole,** podcast host and author of *Everyday Prayers for the School Year*

Our world is in desperate need of true and lasting joy. *Surrender the Joy Stealers* is filled with practical tips to help you not only identify the things that rob you of joy but remove them at their root.
—**Abby McDonald**, author of *Shift*, writing coach, and writer for Proverbs 31 Ministries' Encouragement for Today

Maintaining our joy in turbulent times is no small struggle. Doris Swift bravely dives into this challenge in *Surrender the Joy Stealers: Rediscover the Jesus Joy in You*. "Naming the joy stealers revokes their power," she writes. "A threat must be identified before it can be eliminated." Ms. Swift encourages looking at situations through a biblical perspective, recognizing that our circumstances are not in control—God is in control. "Sometimes God changes our plans so we can follow his." With seasoned wisdom and Scripture-fed prayers, Ms. Swift leads readers to find and keep their Jesus joy. "When we abide in Jesus, we can trust him with the outcome. That is true surrender." This

practical study will have a lasting impact on Jesus followers who want to escape the despair of daily disappointments and plant their feet firmly on the path of joy.
—**Dianne Barker**, speaker, radio host, and author of *I Don't Chase the Garbage Truck down the Street in My Bathrobe Anymore! Organizing for the Maximum Life.*

We all long for joy, but how do we actually grab hold of it? In *Surrender the Joy Stealers*, Doris has outlined six simple steps for us in this practical Bible study to grasp it firmly in our hand, let it take deep root within our heart, and fill us with strength and courage to walk it out. This Bible study is about lasting life change. Don't miss it!
—**Erica Wiggenhorn**, international speaker and author of *An Unexpected Revival: Experiencing God's Goodness Through Disappointment and Doubt,* an eight-week Bible study through the prophecies of Ezekiel.

Surrender the Joy Stealers is a fantastic six-session Bible study by Doris Swift that helps women rediscover their joy and live their best lives. With relatable stories, biblical teachings, and practical tips, this study guides readers to identify and surrender their joy stealers to God. It's perfect for anyone who wants to experience more joy and fulfillment in their lives. Doris is a trustworthy guide, and I highly recommend this important resource!
—**Chad Allen**, writing coach and founder of BookCamp.us

Do day-to-day circumstances, struggles, relationships, and emotions seem to drain every drop of joy from you? I highly recommend you immerse yourself in Doris Swift's new six-week Bible study, *Surrender the Joy Stealers,* as she helps you connect to the One who will renew your joy.

Doris's study will help you identify with what is stealing your joy and discover ways to recover it again through Scripture, prayer practices, and answering thoughtful questions. You'll especially enjoy Doris's way of counseling you through the study with her encouraging words and illustrations.

You'll discover it's like having her in the room with you, leading you to catch the hand of Jesus and a life of joy.

—**Nancy B Booth**, spiritual director, author of *Want to Hear God, Connect with Him in Prayer*

Surrender the Joy Stealers:

Rediscover the Jesus Joy in You
Six-Week Bible Study

Doris Swift

A Christian Company
ElkLakePublishingInc.com

COPYRIGHT NOTICE

Surrender the Joy Stealers: Rediscover the Jesus Joy in You

First edition. Copyright © 2023 by DORIS SWIFT. The information contained in this book is the intellectual property of DORIS SWIFT and is governed by United States and International copyright laws. All rights reserved. No part of this publication, either text or image, may be used for any purpose other than personal use. Therefore, reproduction, modification, storage in a retrieval system, or retransmission, in any form or by any means, electronic, mechanical, or otherwise, for reasons other than personal use, except for brief quotations for reviews or articles and promotions, is strictly prohibited without prior written permission by the publisher.

Unless otherwise indicated, all Scripture quotations are from the ESV® Bible (The Holy Bible, English Standard Version®), copyright © 2001 by Crossway, a publishing ministry of Good News Publishers. Used by permission. All rights reserved.

Scriptures marked (NASB) are taken from the NEW AMERICAN STANDARD BIBLE(R), Copyright (C) 1960,1962,1963,1968,1971,1972,1973,1975,1977,1995 by The Lockman Foundation. Used by permission.

Scripture quotations marked NLT are taken from the *Holy Bible*, New Living Translation, Copyright © 1996, 2004, 2015 by Tyndale House Foundation. Used by permission of Tyndale House Publishers, Inc., Carol Stream, Illinois 60188. All rights reserved.

Cover and Interior Design: Derinda Babcock, Deb Haggerty

Editor(s): Peggy Ellis, Judy Hagey, Deb Haggerty

Author Represented By: The Blythe Daniel Agency

PUBLISHED BY: Elk Lake Publishing, Inc., 35 Dogwood Drive, Plymouth, MA 02360, 2023

Library Cataloging Data

Names: Swift, Doris (Doris Swift)
Surrender the Joy Stealers, Rediscover the Jesus Joy in You / Doris Swift
216 p. 23cm × 15cm (9in × 6 in.)

ISBN-13: 978-1-64949-924-0 (paperback) | 978-1-64949-925-7 (trade hardcover) | 978-1-64949-926-4 (trade paperback) | 978-1-64949-927-1 (e-book)

Key Words: Joy in difficult times; joy; surrender to God; Jesus; living on mission; John 15; discipleship.

Library of Congress Control Number: 2023940350 Nonfiction

TABLE OF CONTENTS

Endorsements ii
Copyright Notice xii
Table of Contents xiii
Foreword xv
Acknowledgments xvii
Introduction xix
How to Use This Study xxi
Week One: Reveal 1
Week Two: Respond 43
Week Three: Receive 77
Week Four: Renew 109
Week Five: Rest 133
Week Six: Reach 151
Leader's Guide 173
About the Author 185
Endnotes 187

FOREWORD

We've lost our joy, friends. Something walked right in, bold as day, and stole it out from underneath us. We are discouraged. We are angry. We are sad. We are confused. We are at odds with each other—and the world is receiving a jaded message about faith. That's not who we are, and that's why I'm saying this bold and clear.

It's time to take our joy back.

There's a price to pay when joy is lost. In Matthew 23, Jesus lists seven woes of people who have lost their joy. When I first read this, I thought he was just talking about a particular group of people, until I realized that woe means sorrow, bleak disappointment, and sadness. Jesus wasn't pointing fingers. He was grieved that his people were living joyless lives, defined by woe. He was teaching his message boldly to usher the crowd away from such bleak faith.

He offered more. He still does.

When I was asked to write this foreword, I was in one of the hardest seasons of my life, but I had also discovered things about joy that took my breath away. I had to redefine it from happiness that goes up and down to the joy Jesus promised. It's not utopian joy that hides her head in the sand. It's not joy that stuffs the hard stuff into the recesses of her heart because they are too painful to face. It's not joy that puts on a mask or pretends. This is joy that is deeply rooted. Joy that is a shelter. Joy that helps us find our place and assignment in the world. Joy that leads us away from joy stealers to live in the truth. Joy that is with us, and in us, even when things are hard.

This kind of joy will break through in a world that feels pretty ominous right now. This kind of joy blankets a home. It blankets a heart. It makes room for real feelings, but also allows Jesus to step into the midst of those emotions.

We understand joy stealers will crop up, but true joy comes as we identify them and embrace our *Source* of joy. The early church exhibited this phenomenon. Joy marked them, and yet they dealt with difficult people, up and down conditions, grief, and loss. They had to work through conflict. They dealt with messy humans. They experienced cultural differences, personalities, and persecution.

They were able to live in joy (not up-and-down happiness, but deeply grounded joy) because they knew where to turn. They knew whose they were. They trusted that God would walk with them, even when the path seemed unclear or rocky. They were tethered to something bigger than themselves or their circumstances.

My prayer is you'll dig deep into the joy stealers in this book, and deeper into the Source of joy who loves, loves, loves you.

—Suzanne Eller, bestselling author of twelve books including *JoyKeeper: 6 Truths that Change Everything You Thought You Knew about Joy*. Host of *Prayer Starters* podcast, and cohost of "More Than Small Talk" with Holley Gerth and Jennifer Watson.

ACKNOWLEDGMENTS

I give thanks to my Lord and Savior, Jesus Christ—apart from you I can do nothing.

To my sweet parents, thank you for raising this God's girl and for your continuous love and support.

To my amazing husband Brian, I adore you, and your love and encouragement mean more to me than you know.

To my dear family, church family, and friends, thank you for cheering me on throughout this book journey. You know who you are, and I am beyond grateful for you.

To my amazing agent, Blythe Daniel, your wisdom, guidance, and uplifting words have blessed me greatly. Thank you for championing this project and seeing it through to fruition.

To Chad R. Allen, thank you for pouring into my writing as a coach and mentor.

To my gifted editor, Peggy Ellis, you have taken these words and made them shine, and I am so thankful for you.

To Deb Haggerty, Judy Hagey, and Elk Lake Publishing, I am grateful for the opportunity to work with you and could not imagine a better home for this study.

To the women who walk this six-week journey, thank you for allowing me to walk beside you.

And to my heavenly Father, thank you for your faithfulness—I am humbled and blessed to be your child.

INTRODUCTION

Welcome to the *Surrender the Joy Stealers* Bible study! My prayer is that in the weeks ahead you will find freedom through surrendering your joy stealers to God, rediscovering the joy Jesus gave you, and walking forward in your calling and purpose. I'm looking forward to our journey together as we delve into God's word and apply his guidance to our lives. We were made for community, and I'm so glad you're here.

Several years ago, I spoke at a women's event about finding joy in our calling. Before guests arrived, women serving at the event placed strips of pink paper and a handful of pens on each table. Midway through my talk, I asked the audience of women to grab a strip of paper and write down everything which threatened to steal their joy—now was the time to surrender them to God. I had no idea how many women would participate, but I knew God was at work. These precious women couldn't grab a paper and pen fast enough, ready to release their burdens in scribbled messages to God. I invited them to come forward and deposit their joy stealers into a box, and in exchange receive a white carnation representing their acceptance of God's joy and peace. Before I could finish the invitation, streams of women from all directions came forward to surrender their joy stealers into that box.

As a leader in women's ministry, I counsel countless women who've forgotten their worth, question their value, and can't find their joy. Have you been there? So have I. When the struggles of this world drain us dry and wring us out, our desert mentality becomes fertile ground for the Enemy's lies to grow. We place our trust in things we see and feel instead of in the God we know. The Enemy might threaten to steal our joy—but the truth is, he can't crack the code. God has infused us with his joy, his Spirit, and his love. We are soaked in his living water that can't be drained dry, and we are filled with his joy that can't be emptied.

Surrender the Joy Stealers is a strategic, six-session Bible study designed to help women like you rediscover the overflowing, ever-present Jesus joy within, that fills you, empowers you, and ripens the fruit God produces in your life. Now is the time to identify your joy stealers, surrender them to God, reawaken the joy within you, and share that joy with others.

HOW TO USE THIS STUDY

Surrender the Joy Stealers is a group study but can also be used for individual study. I highly recommend a group environment because women will be able to encourage one another.

Although this is a six-week study, it could also be expanded to a twelve-week study by stretching each weekly session to two weeks. Group members may appreciate extra time to work on their personal study time between sessions. At the beginning of each week and each day of study, you'll find **Scripture-Fed Prayer for the Journey.** Use the words of the Scripture passage or verse in the form of a prayer. At the end of each week, you'll find a section called **Back to the Vine.** Although our study includes several passages from different books of the Bible, our primary focus is John 15, specifically John 15:11. We always get back to the vine, Jesus, our true vine, who placed his joy in us that our joy may be full.

During the first week, women identify what threatens to steal their joy. When engaging in group study, there's a caveat concerning relationships. *Surrender the Joy Stealers* is meant to be a journey of discovery and personal growth in Christ. If a joy stealer happens to be a spouse/friend/other family member, there is a common desire to see the other person "fixed" and experience transformation. Raw emotions may cause a woman to want to spill out every detail of her relationship issues with the group. During the first meeting, group leaders must communicate that women are encouraged to share while, at the same time, avoiding oversharing about someone outside the group.

In other words, we want our conversations to be seasoned with salt and honoring to the Lord. We can discuss our joy stealers without overstepping boundaries when it comes to our relationships with others. Always allow the Holy Spirit to direct the conversation, and gently redirect the flow back to how God's word provides us with solutions to experience our own transformation. The Bible helps us learn to see our lives and circumstances through a biblical lens, which changes our perspective and brings hope and healing. The other person in a relationship may never choose to change, but God can do a miraculous transformation in and through us, enabling us to experience his gift of joy in all circumstances.

FIERCE CALLING PODCAST

After Back to the Vine, you'll find a "Listen" section. Do you listen to podcasts? I hope you do! I invite you to listen to the *Fierce Calling Podcast*. Each week, I welcome guests to share their stories and how they are acting where their passion, compassion, and conviction intersect—my definition of a fierce calling. They share how God brought them through hard seasons of life and how they are using their gifts to impact the world for Christ.

In the "Listen" section, I point you to specific episodes chosen especially for each week. I provide an abundance of episode options to listen to with guests who span all seasons of life. These conversations will encourage, inspire, and challenge you to act where your passion, compassion, and conviction intersect. I provide the direct link to the podcast player on my website, but you can also find the *Fierce Calling Podcast* most places you listen to podcasts. Don't forget to subscribe so you'll never miss an episode. During each episode, guests also share helpful resources, information about books, and various ministry opportunities. You'll find links to their websites in the weekly show notes.

GROUP SESSIONS AND HOMEWORK

The study is designed for weekly group sessions followed by five days of personal study, aka homework. Please do not let the word homework intimidate you. While completing each day's study work is ideal, it is not a requirement. There is no need to feel discouraged if you have not finished by the next group session. The Enemy wants you to stay home and isolate, but go, even if the dog ate your homework. Finding a time that works best for you, and sticking to that time each day, if possible, might be helpful.

You will find there are thought-provoking questions to allow you to make Scripture connections and discoveries. In some studies, there might be answers after the questions, but in this study, you will discover answers on your own. Bible study encourages us to seek the Spirit's leading in understanding God's word. You'll discover during group time how God reveals things one or more group members needed to hear that day. That is the beauty of community. God never changes and his word never changes. We are the ones who experience transformative change through his word.

The first session is an opportunity to get to know the others in your group. If you're the group leader, you might ask each woman to share a little about herself and what she hopes to get out of the study. Light snacks might be provided, but please do not feel obligated to offer a smorgasbord. We're trying to surrender our joy stealers, not create more of them, amen? Perhaps the women in the group can take turns bringing healthy snacks.

Study Tips

The Bible verses in this study are taken primarily from the English Standard Version (ESV), but I encourage you to cross reference verses in multiple versions. There are several free online resources where you can view multiple versions of Scripture side-by-side. Biblegateway.com, Biblehub.com, and Blueletterbible.org are a few. The New Living Translation (NLT) and the New American Standard Bible (NASB) are great options for cross referencing verses. Use the version you prefer, and other versions to reinforce your understanding of the word.

Commentaries can be helpful resources as well. However, I suggest praying before studying and asking the Holy Spirit to bring you fresh revelation and understanding. Allow God to teach and guide you through his word first, then reference outside resources for additional insights.

Group Leader Tips:

Begin and end on time
- Open with prayer (This is a Bible study, not a prayer meeting, so decide how to manage prayer requests)
- Establish the need for confidentiality within the group
- Encourage group participation to share as women feel led
- Create an environment where all group members have an opportunity to share
- Invite group members to share insights God has revealed to them during their study time

- Use the "Back to the Vine" section at the end of each study week for additional talking points. Ask group members to share what they gleaned from the *Fierce Calling Podcast* episodes.

WEEK ONE: REVEAL

IDENTIFYING YOUR JOY STEALERS

Introduction: Naming Your Joy Stealers and Redefining Your Circumstances

Scripture-fed prayer for the journey: John 15:1–11

When was the last time you felt safe sharing your deepest wounds and darkest secrets? Remember the women's event I mentioned in the Introduction to the book when women dropped their joy stealers into a box? There was nothing extraordinary about that box, but there was something extraordinary about their act of surrender. The authors of those notes were anonymous, but that didn't matter. God knew them and wanted them to know that somebody cared.

> *Because sometimes what we need most is for someone to listen to and validate our pain.*

After the event, I wept as I sat on the living room floor reading and praying for each woman represented in the box of joy stealers. Each one represented a painful season plagued by heartache. By the time I was finished, I'd rounded the corner to a full-on ugly cry. My husband didn't know whether to console me or run.

I expected things like chaotic schedules, comparison, worry—we all struggle with those valid joy stealers. Yet there is something about anonymity that makes us brave enough to share the joy stealers we dare not speak aloud—the ones wrapped in shame that bear the stigma of a condemning world. Joy stealers like broken marriages, abusive relationships, alcoholism, addictions, self-hatred. Then there was this one: LIFE.

LIFE in screaming caps, period. My heart broke for her, and I didn't even know her name, but God did. He knows your name and mine too and he calls us by it.

> But now, this is what the Lord says, *He who is* your Creator, Jacob, And He who formed you, Israel: 'Do not fear, for I have redeemed you; I have called you by name; you are Mine! (Isaiah 43:1 NASB)

The woman who wrote LIFE? I pray she left that event with more than just a fresh carnation. I pray she left with a fresh perspective on life, knowing her life has purpose and meaning. Life can be a devastating journey when storms blow in, but our joy stealers do not define us. God formed us, and he defines us through Christ. Our devastation becomes our destiny if we allow the joy stealers to steer our ships, which isn't God's design for us. We can name our joy stealers and discover how God renames our purpose when we abide in him.

Could you use a fresh perspective on life? Let's begin this week expecting to receive it.

Day One

Revealing What Threatens to Steal Your Joy

Naming Your Joy Stealers and Revoking Their Power Over You

Scripture-fed Prayer for the Journey:

Read Psalm 91 adding your name and allowing each verse to guide you in a personal prayer to God.
Now let's read John 15:4.
Where do we want to be?

Reread Psalm 91:1

Where do we want to be?

Both these verses remind us not only where we want to be but also where we want to stay—secure and connected to God. As we go through these weeks together, let us always come back to this important truth.

Reveal their Names—Revoke their Power

The day began like any other workday at the bank I managed. A coworker alerted me to the masked men wielding weapons just a stone's throw away from our desks. She tapped on the glass partition between us and pointed toward the teller line. My mind struggled to comprehend what my eyes were seeing, a towering figure aiming the barrel of his threat at the tellers as his accomplice jumped the counter and filled a sack with cash. Then, in a matter of minutes, the pair of joy stealers dashed out of the building and zoomed off—oblivious to the trauma left behind.

I pulled the robbery kit from the drawer and handed each coworker a description sheet. We wrote down anything we could recall: hair color, eye color, moles, tattoos ... anything to help the police identify the joy stealers who came calling that day.

A threat must be identified before it can be eliminated.

We must expose anything threatening to steal our joy—name it and bring it into the light. We can ask the Holy Spirit to reveal what ails our souls when we can't put our finger on the reason. Ephesians 5:13 tells us anything exposed by the light becomes visible. Although the bank robbers were a visible threat, sometimes our greatest fears stem from invisible threats—the ones we need to allow the light of Christ in us to shine on and expose. Through this, we will overcome those threats through Christ who strengthens us to face our fears.

Revealing our joy stealers is the first step in revoking their power over us.

As we journey together through this week's study time, know this—God journeys with us.

> It is the LORD who goes before you. He will be with you; he will not leave you or forsake you. Do not fear or be dismayed. (Deuteronomy 31:8)

Naming Your Joy Stealers

What Threatens to Steal Your Joy?

Take time to pray before answering this important question, and if you can't put your finger on the problem, ask the Holy Spirit to reveal it to you. He might reveal something you had not realized or considered before now.

Place a check mark beside all that apply, then read the applicable Scripture provided.

_____The threat to my joy is something I have done. (Read Exodus 2:11–15)

_____The threat to my joy is something that has been done to me. (Read 2 Samuel 13)

_____The threat to my joy is something God can help me change. (Read Luke 19:1–10)

_____The threat to my joy is something only God can change. (Matthew 9:20–22)

How do each of the following passages apply to the above statements?

Exodus 2:11–15

2 Samuel 13

Luke 19:1–10

Matthew 9:20–22

Did reading those passages change your perspective on your own joy stealers? If so, explain your new perspective below:

God was in each biblical account named above. He witnessed Moses' poor choices, he was with Tamar in her trauma, he changed the heart of Zacchaeus, and he healed the woman with the issue of blood. God never abandons us in our pain, even when seemingly, he is absent. God is never absent which means he is not only with us in our pain, he also sees and knows the cause of it.

People might falsely believe a Christian will never face pain, suffering, struggles, challenges, tragedy. That's not true, and God never said it was. In John 16:33, Jesus told us we would have trouble in this world. He tells us to take heart because he has overcome the world, which means even though this world is broken because of sin, in him we are victorious because he was victorious over death.

People might also believe that, when Christians go through a trial, they must be lacking in faith or perhaps they have unconfessed or unforgiven sin. While sin causes us a world of trouble, not all the trouble we experience is because of our sin.

Read John 9:1–3. How did Jesus answer his disciples?

I'm so sorry for your pain if you have yet to be physically healed. There is no easy way to explain these difficult seasons, except our temporary home is in a fallen and broken world. Like the blind man Jesus spoke of, God can use physical issues for his glory. Healing might not come as fast as we'd like, or look as we think it should look, but whether our faith is strong or weak, God can use every ounce of pain and suffering for his glory and for the furtherance of his kingdom.

Perhaps you have suffered a traumatic experience and need emotional and spiritual healing. I want to encourage you to believe that God desires to mend your broken heart and bind up your wounds. Pray for God to reveal where he was when you went through this experience. He wants to show you he never left you. He wants to comfort you in your pain, and help you work through your healing process, whether that be physically, mentally, spiritually, emotionally, or all the above.

The Beauty of the Vine, the Vinedresser, and the Branches

As we talked about in the Introduction, God calls us by name, and in John 15, Jesus calls us by another name—branch.

Read John 15:5–6.

What do we learn about our role as a branch in verse 5?

What do we learn about the verse 6 branches?

Who is the true vine John 15:1 speaks of?

Who is the vinedresser in John 15:1?

Isn't the triune picture of the vine, the vinedresser, and us a beautiful one? We as a branch are brought into community with Jesus, the life-giving vine, and the vinedresser, our loving Father, who prunes us by hand, cutting back whatever produces less fruit in us, so in due time, he can produce abundant fruit. Pruning might sound anything but loving, but be assured, those things our Father removes from our lives are not to punish us, but so we might flourish. If you garden, you understand. Good gardeners carefully and meticulously prune everything which delights them and brings them joy—resulting in a sight to behold when new blooms appear in fruitful abundance. Pruning might be God helping us break free of our joy stealers—perhaps a relationship, a stronghold, pride, or a wrong done to us we need to forgive. When God does the pruning, we can trust it is for our good.

We want to be pruned because our Father delights in us and desires we bear much fruit. Thankfully, we're not in charge of producing the fruit. God is. Our role is to be willing and obedient to God's call, a willing branch abiding in the vine.

In Isaiah, we see the outcome of God withdrawing his favor and presence and withholding his pruning.

Read Isaiah 5:4–6. Record below any references to fruit, pruning, and devastation of the land:

Israel had turned from God to worship false gods. After King Solomon's death, the kingdom of God's people split in two—the northern kingdom of Israel and the southern kingdom of Judah with Jerusalem as its capital. Disputes, disagreements, and drama plagued them. They would both face a dismal fate because of their disobedience and turning away from the God who loved them.

The kingdom of Israel fell first because of disobedience and sinful behavior. Destroyed and taken into captivity by the Assyrians, the northern kingdom experienced the removal of God's presence. We learn Judah would suffer similar destruction years later at the hands of the Babylonians. Thankfully, a remnant of his people was saved, and out of that line, Jesus the Messiah would come.

Friend, we want to be pruned, and we want to be the John 15:5 branches—believing, trusting, and receiving all God has and desires to give us. We want to abide in the true vine—Jesus.

We are branches who abide in him and are made righteous through his sacrifice on the cross. Jesus is our example, and as we grow in him, we become more like him. He goes before us and shows us the way. Jesus was the Righteous Branch before we became branches made righteous in him.

In Isaiah 4:2, how is the branch described?

What is the pride and honor of the survivors of Israel?

Isaiah 11:1 says, "There shall come forth a shoot from the stump of Jesse, and a branch from his roots shall bear fruit." Jesse was King David's father, a man of lowly means, which is likely represented in the humble beginnings and humanity of Jesus. God's promise to David was that from his offspring, long after he was gone, the Messiah would come. Jesus is referred to as the Son of David, but we must remember David was the son of Jesse, the place where Jesus was the Righteous Branch who sprouted from a stump, a seemingly lifeless stump. The Branch who sprang forth from a seemingly dead tree stump is the source of hope for the world (see Jeremiah 23:5).

We need to know our role as the branch because as we go through John 15, we learn we can do nothing as a branch apart from the vine. Abiding in the vine helps us surrender our joy stealers because our role is not to control and fix everything, even though as women we try, don't we? We need Jesus to help us surrender—the step we take in Week Two.

Naming our joy stealers is the beginning of renaming our circumstances. Renaming our circumstances means looking at the situation through a biblical perspective.

When we change our perspective to God's perspective regarding our current circumstances, hopeless becomes hopeful, and the overwhelmed can overcome because God is sovereign, able, and in control. Our circumstances are redefined when we define who is truly in control.

Our circumstances cannot control us because God is in control.

Today you took an important step in naming your joy stealers, because identification cancels personification, which is when we give human characteristics to non-human things like emotions, for example. Emotions such as fear, worry, and anxiety are often described as gripping, suffocating, consuming—something we struggle with, fight against, and battle. Although these emotions can and do cause physical responses, they cannot physically respond to us. God can. Doesn't that bring a level of comfort to your soul?

You are a vibrant branch connected to Jesus, the true vine. Hold tightly to that truth.

Day Two

Revealing Unhealthy Emotions

*Naming What's Really Behind
Your Worry, Fear, Guilt, Shame*

Scripture-fed prayer for the journey: Read Psalm 91

In 1981, my mother, sister, and I agreed to set an alarm for 4:30 a.m. to witness a major event—Princess Diana's royal wedding. Although much has changed within the British monarchy and its authority over the years, loyal citizens under a reigning king or queen consider themselves subject to their authority. The Prime Minister is the head of the British government; however, it is still customary to bow to the King or Queen of England as an expression of deep respect and honor.

What in our lives causes us to bow? What do we allow to reign over us? Emotions are essential in our lives, and God gave us emotions, but at times we feel like they rule us, amen? When putting our emotions into perspective, we need not be subject to them, nor bow down to them. When we bow to our emotions, they can become idols in our lives, and before we know it, we're falling into the sin-trap the Enemy set for us. When we allow anger to dominate us, fear to paralyze us, worry to overcome us, and shame to isolate us, in essence, we're placing them before God in our lives instead of bringing them before God on our knees.

List any emotions you are currently feeling.

Analyze the cause for each emotion you listed above. Can you identify the source or reason for what you're feeling? If so, pray about it. If not, pray about it. Often, we might find it easier to have isolate, wallow-in-defeat kinds of reactions than to fight for soul-healthy, positive ones—but those are unhealthy responses. Talk to God about what you're feeling, and allow his peace to wash over you.

We will talk more about how to surrender our emotions to God in Week Two, but for now, hang on to this truth:

Emotional health comes by applying
God's word to our circumstances.

Emotional healing comes by relying on
God's word to rename our circumstances.

Of course, self-control might not always be cut and dry. Emotions, depression for example, can weigh heavily, and seeking a professional, godly counselor might be a wise choice for you.

The good news is many emotions we experience daily are positive ones—let's allow them to speak louder in our lives, outshining those negative ones.

OUR EMOTIONS MIGHT STEM FROM PAST PAIN

Many emotions can stem from past trauma and pain, including guilt, shame, insecurity, worry, fear. We might not realize something from our past still steers our emotions. For example, children who are continually told they are stupid will come to believe they really are, and that lie can stick with them throughout adulthood. Every time they make a mistake, they'll attribute the error to being stupid, because that's what they've been conditioned to believe. Words matter. What we say and what we hear matters. We can change the trajectory of someone's life, or even our own lives, by replacing that lie with the truth of God's word.

When you think back on your childhood memories, what types of emotions do those memories invoke?

What is your fondest childhood memory or family tradition?

What is your most painful childhood or young adult memory?

What is your most painful memory as an adult?

Painful memories can be the loss of a loved one, something we've done, or something that's been done to us—or even all three. Perhaps there are generational sin patterns we need the Lord to help us overcome. We abide in the true vine for this reason. Jesus is our lifeline vine. He holds our hands through the root-pulling journey when we face hard things from our past, those things we've stuffed so deep down they've taken root.

Read Isaiah 41:10–13 and note below what stands out to you:

God is encouraging his people—we are his people too. I especially love that God holds us by our right hands.

What is the significance of the right hand? Read the following verses and record what the right hand signifies:

Psalm 63:8

Psalm 45:9

Genesis 48:13–19

Ephesians 1:19–21

God holds our hands through every hard experience and relives every hard experience with us so the healing process can begin. He is with us in the pit of despair and the valley of sorrows because even when he feels far from us, truth tells us he is near.

Fill in the blanks of this verse below from Psalm 34:18:

The LORD is _____ to the _____

and _____ the_____ in spirit.

We all have them, those gloomy, broken parts of our stories we try hiding in the back of our closets; painful memories dressed in shame. Jesus already dealt with our shame. He shamed shame on the cross. Being crucified was considered such a shameful execution, Romans would not permit their own criminals to be crucified on a cross. When shame plagues us it's as if we're saying Jesus's crucifixion was not enough. That realization was eye-opening for me, and I hope it is for you. What Jesus did on the cross for you and for me was more than enough.

Jesus shamed shame, and we are shameless in his name.

God created us with emotions. Positive emotions flow from a joyful heart, a feeling of contentment. Joy-stealing negative emotions—shame, jealousy, fear, hatred, unforgiveness—can become toxic to our souls and to others around us. When we feel them, we can choose to glorify God by surrendering them to him.

When our emotions accelerate into overdrive, we need to be aware of downward-spiral-thinking. Thoughts like 'there's no hope, I'm not going to make it through this, I can't face another day' can become toxic to our mental health. We've all struggled with emotions run amok, but we're not called to do this life alone. God created us for community, and that includes when we need to reach for help. He directs us and guides us when joy stealers get so close that we can feel their hot breath on our necks.

Awareness of our emotions is key. Negative emotions are red-flag warning signs. Just like smoke detectors warn us of fire, negative emotions warn us we're heading down a possible path of destruction. Psalm 16:11 tells us God will show us the path of life, and not just any life, an abundant life. God can help us redirect our steps and follow the path he has paved for us.

We Are Empowered by the Spirit

Life is busy, hard, and hectic, and we forget the empowerment God has given us, don't we? The empowerment by the Spirit we've had since the day we met Jesus. He placed his Spirit in us to empower us for our calling, and he placed his joy in us, that our joy might be full (see John 15:11). We have the same Spirit within us as the one who raised Jesus from the grave. When we grasp that truth, there are no limits to what God can do in and through us for his glory.

God's empowerment is not all we forget. We also forget there's an Enemy of our soul—the chief joy stealer.

Read John 10:10.

What does the thief come to do?

If you left out the word *only,* go back and add it. Circle it. The only purpose on the thief's daily agenda is to steal, kill, and destroy. Many Bible scholars and commentators note the "thief" in this verse is referencing false prophets who "steal" away the truth from hearers. Ultimately, the thief is the Enemy. He wants our joy because he knows that without it, we lose focus on our purpose. He wants us bound in despair and oppression so we can't fulfill our calling—so we can't share our grace story and tell others about how Jesus transformed our lives.

Why does it matter that we know this?

Satan wants to kidnap us from our true family—he goes after our joy, so we'll forget who we are. Yet we cannot lose our joy or our hope because we can't lose our Jesus, the source of both. Sometimes we're our own worst enemy, aren't we? We make our own messes like a toddler scattering Legos across the floor, and eventually, our bare feet step on them in the dark. Sin always leads to pain—and no matter how hard we try justifying it or disguising it, sooner or later, we step on those Legos. Sin has a ripple effect in addition to our pain. People walking in sin, including us, will tell others to mind their own business. The problem is, our sin hurts others too, and their sins can hurt us. If those Legos aren't cleaned up, we're not the only ones who'll step on them in the dark. We become vulnerable if we think we're good and will never fall into sin.

Read 1 Peter 5:8, 1 John 1:8, and Romans 3:23.
What do these verses tell us?

Now read Romans 6:10–14
What do these verses tell us?

We can't fight the Enemy on our own. The good news is, we're not alone. We have God's love, grace, peace, and power within us, and he is with us.

WE CAN CHOOSE WHAT WE ALLOW

Here's some encouragement—we have a choice. We can allow our emotions to lead us down the wrong path, like stuffing the nearest brownie for comfort, lashing out with words we can't take back, drinking away the pain, and the list goes on. We do these things to dull something we are perhaps meant to feel. Instead, we can choose to allow God to do a work on our hearts and the root causes of our emotional outbursts. He is our vinedresser after all. He wants to prune us branches and clean out everything which needs to be released from our lives. We want to remain in Jesus—our true vine—and be the branches who abide in the firm foundation of his roots.

Picture two neighbors tending their lawns. One neighbor's lawn is a lush blanket of emerald with no weeds in sight, while the other neighbor's lawn, although neatly mowed, is dotted with weeds, starving the good grass of needed nutrients. Weeds spread like wildfire and can overtake an entire lawn in a flash. Although both neighbors mow their lawns and water their grass, there is one critical difference—the neighbor with the healthy lawn kills the weeds at their roots. Merely chopping off weed growth won't rid the lawn of the menacing pestilence. Weeds must be pulled at the roots.

Weeding out negative emotions calls for pulling their destructive roots from the good soil.

God gave us emotions, and we know he has emotions too. Read these verses and list the emotions attributed to God in each one:

Romans 5:8

Isaiah 62:5

Psalm 135:14

Psalm 7:11

Proverbs 6:16

Matthew 26:38

John 11:35

There are an abundance of Scripture verses expressing God's emotions. He feels for us and loves us. He is our example, and whether we experience positive or negative emotions, the key is how we handle them and our resulting action.

For example, when God is angry as in Psalm 7:11, his anger does not lead to sin because there is no sin in God. However, his displeasure can result in consequences meant for the good of a person or people. Anger might be viewed as a negative emotion, but anger is not a sin, according to the word of God and his example. Ephesians 4:26 warns us we should not sin while angry. The Enemy will use our anger to tempt us into taking actions we'll likely regret later. Awareness of our emotions opens our eyes to deeper things in our lives. Emotions are our internal temperature check of what's going on in our souls.

> ***Healthy emotions help us feel something; negative emotions help us reveal something.***

What happens to our God-given joy when we go through a difficult season? We have full permission to experience joy at all seasons of our lives.

> ***Joy might not change our circumstances, but we have permission to experience our God-given joy without guilt or shame.***

Let's acknowledge the power of God's joy in us. His joy makes our joy full, overriding the brokenness of this world and the devastation of our circumstances. We are supernaturally filled with joy and have permission to experience it in all the seasons of our lives, not just the good ones. Allow that truth to sink in and encourage your heart today.

Day Three

Revealing Struggles with Relationships

Naming Your Relationship Conflicts and the Need for Boundaries

Scripture-fed prayer for the journey: Pray Psalm 91 and this time, instead of adding your name, add the name of a person with whom you have a struggling relationship. Pray God will reveal nuggets of truth to you as we work through Day Three.

Read John 15:9–10. What is the main theme these verses talk about?

People will fail us but God is there for us without fail

"I just got a call. My brother's baby died." I was stunned and saddened by my fiancé's words. I was even more stunned when I learned it wasn't true. Relationships can be messy, and we have permission to define healthy boundaries with others. God ended that relationship for my good even though I didn't realize it at the time.

Are you currently in a difficult relationship with a spouse, family member, or friend?

If so, what are the main struggles as you see them?

As Christians, we are called to love everyone, yes, *everyone*. Let's be real—love is not always easy. Loving others well does not negate our need to be loved well by others. In a difficult relationship that might not always be the case. When we experience a broken relationship in our lives, remember God sees all and knows every detail. There might be times when seeking wise counsel from a trusted mentor or counselor is necessary. There is no shame in seeking outside help, so please revoke the power any shamers might have over you. Asking for help is a sign of strength, not weakness.

> *Nobody gets to shame you because*
> *Jesus conquered shame on the cross.*

Not every Christian agrees with the need for counseling. How then do we explain those who are called to counsel others? God not only provided the Holy Spirit as our helper, and not only do we have Jesus as our Wonderful Counselor, but there are also instructions in the Bible about seeking wise counsel.

Read Proverbs 1:5 and 19:20. Paraphrase these verses in your own words below.

Wise counsel is ultimately from God. A true follower of Christ seeks God's wisdom and direction when counseling others. The Holy Spirit helps those being counseled to discern the counsel received and how they might apply it in everyday life.

FAMILY TIES THAT BIND

Raise your hand if you grew up in a family that kept struggles hidden from the outside world. If this is you, don't feel alone—many of us are raising our hands with you. Hiding struggles tends to be a cultural thing and almost a family pact that whatever happens at home, stays at home. Yet the very core of the family unit can split like firewood while keeping up appearances. Eventually, the inner workings crumble, and by then, brokenness and pain are deeply ingrained in the family's DNA. There's good news. Jesus came to free us from the bondage of generational sin and continuous cycles of wounding. People are far from perfect, and when we've been hurt by a betrayal of trust, God grieves with us and walks through it with us.

BETRAYAL CUTS DEEP BUT GOD'S LOVE GOES DEEPER

God can wipe away pain and hurt without a trace, but sometimes we learn more through suffering.

Read 1 Peter 5:10; 2 Corinthians 4:1; and Romans 5:2–5
What do these verses tell us about suffering?

God is near in our suffering, and he binds our wounds. We need his heavenly salve for deep healing, and sometimes, we need our scars to remain. Our scars are reminders of God's faithfulness in bringing us through a storm, and God gets all the glory because in John 15:5, Jesus tells us apart from him we can do nothing.

Sometimes God changes our plans so we can follow his.

Like the fiancé who was not the person God meant for me, we can trust God will expose the lies. We can almost hear him say, "No, this is not my plan for you. I have something better in mind."

WHEN OUR CHILDREN ARE STRUGGLING

"But I have nowhere to go!" My son's words tore a piece of my heart straight out of my chest. As he walked away from our home that night, even now, some twenty years later, I can hardly bear the thought of it. Although he was no longer a child, your kid is always your kid, even when tough love means experiencing consequences. I blamed myself because, surely, I was an epic failure mom. Mom-guilt plagued me for years, stealing my joy and sticking its shaming finger in my face. I resisted any presence of joy in my life—feeling guilty and undeserving. However, God is faithful, and now, when I look at my son, a husband and father with two amazing kids, I can see how he was at work.

It's hard to feel joy when our children are struggling. You might be living that experience right now or something similar.

***Tough love is tough for everyone involved,
but necessary for everyone's good.***

I can relate if a joy stealer you named in Day One was about a child or children. We moms want only the best for our kids, and we try our best to train them up, but we must trust God with the outcome. There comes a day when we are no longer responsible for the choices our children make. Accepting that fact doesn't mean we love them less, but it probably means we pray for them with even more fervor. We can be there for them when they make mistakes, and so will our heavenly Father, who loves them more than we do. In Week Two, we talk more about surrendering our kids.

WHEN WE'VE BEEN VIOLATED

In Junior High, there was a boy who flattered me even when I felt like a speck in the shadow of the popular girls. He arranged a meeting for us after school. When I say he revealed things I should not have seen, you can imagine my innocence swirling the drain and disappearing into the sewer pipe. The Enemy will use anyone to gain our trust, then steal it. I experienced such shame, and I had done nothing wrong.

If you feel shame, guilt, or find forgiving hard, running toward Jesus is the answer. He offers freedom, healing, and helps us forgive beyond our capacity. Forgiving an undeserving person doesn't make sense in the world today. Some might believe forgiveness lessens the offense and causes more pain. In God's economy, forgiveness equals freedom. Forgiveness doesn't lessen an offense—it frees us from the offender. Jesus became a living sacrifice for us, even though we didn't deserve it either. We can forgive because he first forgave us.

God can take repulsive and offensive acts toward us and flip them. He helps, heals, and holds us close. He restores, resurrects, and reveals a new thing in our lives.

> Behold, I am doing a new thing; now it springs forth, do you not perceive it? I will make a way in the wilderness and rivers in the desert. (Isaiah 43:19)

He makes rivers in the deserts of our dry broken roads and leads us in a new direction. Whether God restores relationships or removes them from our lives, we can trust his action is always for our good and his glory

Pray about who you need to forgive, who you need to ask for forgiveness, and what relationships should remain in your life. Is a relationship broken because of pride? We might not have considered this before, but sometimes our own pride can cause issues in our relationships. We can also ask God to prepare us for things we will learn about ourselves, even if it's not pretty.

Day Four

Revealing the Cracks in Our Jars

Naming Your Physical Pain and How God Can Use It

Scripture-fed prayer for the journey: Read Psalm 91 and today, write out what verses 14–16 mean to you.

Read John 15:7–8.

When we take our place as a branch connected and grafted in the true vine, our desires become that which God desires for us. What we truly desire might surprise us.

God's Truth is Not Dependent on Life's Struggles

"You have a mass on your liver." The voice on the other end of the line was so very nonchalant as the statement rolled off her tongue—except she was talking about my life. Illness, chronic pain, surgeries, and the like can plague these earthly bodies, but they can't displace our internal joy. I didn't know how my story would end, and I waited for days for answers. During that time, all kinds of scenarios invaded my thoughts. Will I need a liver transplant? Is it cancer? Is my liver failing? Will I swell from medications? Will I lose my hair? All valid questions stemming from one single statement.

I think the word that slapped me square in the face was *mass*. Doesn't mass mean massive, as in huge? I didn't hear the measurements she gave, I only heard that one word—*mass*.

In the days that followed, the darkness of an unknown future felt thick like tar—my feet stuck deep in the muck of uncertainty. Still, I knew whatever the outcome, God would be there.

Turns out, the mass was approximately 1.5–2.0 centimeters—about one-half or three-quarters of an inch at most. Several weeks later, tests revealed the mass was a harmless hemangioma—a benign cluster of red blood vessels. I praise God for a good report. However, you might have received a different kind of report. Only God has all the answers, but we can be sure of this, he is faithful, he is with us, and his plans for us are good—he is good.

Read Jeremiah 29:11. What is the promise this verse reveals?

I won't pretend to understand the physical pain you might be going through or offer trite answers neatly wrapped and tied with a bow. Perhaps your journey finds you walking through cancer, arthritis, fibromyalgia, or other debilitating and often devastating physical conditions. We might not understand the whys but there are things we do know about the who—not the band from the seventies, but the one true God, who loves us, cares for us, and sees our pain. That truth stands even amid our struggles.

Read Exodus 20:21 and complete the sentence below.
God met Moses in ...

Read 1Peter 2:9
Who called you?

Where did he call you out of?

What did he call you into?

Friend, God meets us in the thick darkness of our pain and calls us into his wonderful light. He is no stranger to suffering, and our suffering can draw us closer to Christ and, also, glorify him.

Read 1 Peter 4:12–13 and paraphrase these verses:

Jesus never promised a trouble-free, suffer-free, problem-free world—in fact, these are part of the brokenness of living in the aftermath of the fall—that first act of disobedience carried out amidst the beauty of the Garden of Eden. In God's original plans for creation, there was no suffering, shame, pain, loss, or sin. Still, we are living an amazing love story. God loves us, and God himself is love. The purpose of this study is finding the joy you already have so it can flourish, even amid less-than-joyful circumstances. Regardless of circumstances, we can still experience supernatural joy—the joy Jesus gave us—his joy so ours might be full.

*Joy in suffering is not an oxymoron—
it's a purposeful mission of love.*

Some people might say Christ could endure extreme suffering for us because he is God. However, Jesus suffered pain within the confines of flesh with all the nerve-endings and pain sensors we have. He was fully human and experienced horrific human suffering. Luke 22:44 tells us Jesus experienced such anguish and agony as he prayed in the garden of Gethsemane that his sweat was like drops of blood. The medical condition for this is called hematohidrosis and documented cases since have been observed in those who have suffered severe stress or a shock to their system. Jesus was flogged, tearing his flesh and likely exposing bone and muscle. Blood loss was excessive, and people often died from this form of torture alone. Crucifixion is a slow, painful death—the most horrific form of torture we could imagine yet Psalm 147:3 tells us Jesus came to bind our wounds. He does not diminish our suffering in the face of his. Hebrews 12:2 tells us that for the joy set before him he endured the cross. His joy was about us—that by his sacrifice, we would be reconciled in relationship with our Father and become children of God.

This study is not about a theological debate since we know Christians have differing views on sickness, disease, and healing. This study is to glorify God and focus on joy. Joy is a healing balm—a fruit of the Spirit—a supernatural experience the world cannot duplicate. In Week Two, we surrender our pain, but for this week, let us meditate on what we know is true—God is aware when his children are hurting, and he gives us his joy that our joy might be full. We are empowered to endure with joy.

> being strengthened with all power, according to his glorious might, for all endurance and patience with joy;
> (Colossians 1:11)

During today's study time, allow the following Bible verses to fill your heart with joy. Pray them aloud, asking God to help you believe and embrace his healing power and love with your whole heart. Our pain draws us closer to the cross, and through Christ's pain and suffering, our pain and suffering can make him known.

Write a short description of how each of the verses on the next page encourage you.

Psalm 5:11

Psalm 6:2

Jeremiah 17:14

Jeremiah 33:6

Isaiah 53:5

2 Corinthians 12:7–9

We do not understand and cannot explain away all we experience while living in these earthly bodies. Only God has the answers, and we may trust him in sickness and in health.

DAY FIVE

REVEALING THE BROKENNESS OF SELF

Naming Your True Identity and Why It's Important to Remember Who You Are

Scripture-fed prayer for the journey: Read Psalm 139 as a personal prayer.

Next, read John 15:3 and complete the blank line.

Already you are _____

BE WHO YOU ARE

Mandy Mason wanted to deck me, and rumor had it, she etched her plans with a sharp object into a desktop during second period English. The reason? A boy—but I bet you guessed that.

Mandy made it known she was not happy about me going to the Friday night football game with her ex-boyfriend. That was my first experience with bullying, and thankfully, I think it was my last. Mandy's ex-boyfriend arrived at the game with me then left with her—clearly dropping the "ex" from his title. Believe me, I was relieved and decided they deserved each other.

Just when I thought, phew, this whole Mandy thing was over, something unexpected happened—Mandy and I became friends. Well, not BFFs, but friends. Turns out, she wasn't the bully I thought she was. Mandy was creative, artsy, and amazingly talented. When I met the real her, I liked the real her. How often do we do that—miss out on knowing someone because of what we think we know. I thought Mandy was a bully, and that she was mean and hateful. I saw Mandy through her threats, but they weren't the real her.

Circumstances stemming from a broken world can keep us from seeing people for who they really are. I'm not making excuses for negative or sinful behavior, but behaviors stem from what's going on in the heart. If we're honest, there are times we keep people from seeing who we really are—but maybe that's because we struggle with our own identity. Oftentimes, our own sinful behavior stems from an identity crisis.

CLEAN HANDS AND PURE HEARTS

> Who shall ascend the hill of the LORD? And who shall stand in his holy place? He who has clean hands and a pure heart, who does not lift up his soul to what is false and does not swear deceitfully. (Psalm 24:3-4)

When the entire world experiences a pandemic, the most common phrase the entire world hears is "wash your hands." That phrase can be a great reminder for us to own up to our own brokenness—because we may be blaming others for the dirt on our hands.

Sinfulness leads to brokenness while righteousness leads to godliness.

We're all sinners, and in Christ, we're saved by grace, washed clean, and dressed up white as snow like the bride we are. The bride of Christ—the church.

As young girls, my sister, friends, and I loved making mudpies in an imaginary bakeshop behind my garage. We'd play for hours, scooping up dirt with our bare hands and plopping this special ingredient into old coffee cans. The recipe was easy, just add water from the hose, stir with a twig, and you've got yourself a heap of mudpie batter to pour into your Easy Bake Oven pie tins. Our play-clothes started out clean but were soon a dirty mess with mud-smeared faces to match. We wouldn't dare dress up in our Sunday-best to make mudpies—and that makes perfect sense to us, doesn't it?

When we accepted Christ, we became his bride, washed clean. But our flesh? That's another story. Our flesh has a hankering for mudpies. In Galatians 5:24, Paul tells us when we belong to Christ, we've crucified our flesh and nailed sinful passions and desires to the cross, but as we know, brokenness can drag us back behind the garage to scoop up more dirt. Our free-will-choices-with-a-side-of-temptation lead to addictions, infidelity, gossip, promiscuity, and other joy-stealing behaviors derailing God's plans for his daughters. Anything we allow to sit on the throne of our hearts in God's place threatens to steal our joy.

While we're probably not worshipping false gods or golden calves in the backyard, we can unwittingly worship careers, obligations, and anything else that blurs our spiritual eyesight and steals away our time with God. Even our families can become idols to us when they absorb every ounce of our attention.

We must first come clean about our sins, if we want to be made clean. We can receive God's forgiveness and, through him alone, possess the courage which forgiveness toward others requires. We can also forgive ourselves of the past mistakes we've made—those dirty, mudpie mistakes that led to the sin the Enemy keeps trying to smear across our faces. When he tries digging up dirt on us, we can remember this:

> ***The Enemy can't forge a smear campaign with sin for which we've been forgiven.***

As children of God, daughters of the King, the bride of Christ, we are forgiven, and we are sojourners together.

We are becoming the fully healed, healthy disciples we were created to be, who make disciples and use our gifts to impact the world.

Do you believe that not only for others but also for yourself?

If you don't, now is the time. Breathe deeply and rest lovingly in God's perfect peace. In Christ you have been made new, but what does "in Christ" mean?

Let's begin by reading Jeremiah 1:5 and write the verse below.

God's plan for us is to stand on his solid ground. When we understand our identity comes from God, we realize our firm foundation is found in Christ. Something intricately wonderful and miraculously purposeful happens when we accept Christ as our Savior. We are *reborn* or *born again* and as Jesus told Nicodemus in John 3:3, we can't see the kingdom of God unless we are born again.

What does it mean to be born again? This rebirth encompasses these three things:

1. Justification—This happens the moment we accept Christ as our Savior—God's plan of escaping the penalty of sin. Justification came to us by faith and didn't cost us a thing but cost Jesus his life—and because of Jesus's work on the cross—God now sees us as righteous and perfect through his son. This is a state we can refer to as "past complete." Done. We are

justified by faith—it's our position. We are declared righteous and reconciled to a relationship with God (2 Corinthians 5:21). This is our new identity.
2. Sanctification—This is our "present condition." Sanctification simply means we are being set apart for the plans God has and the purposes for those plans. Sanctification is a daily process. We have an escape from the power of sin through Jesus's work on the cross and by growing in Christ each day. "By this will, we have been sanctified through the offering of the body of Jesus Christ once for all time" (Hebrews 10:10 NASB). We are being rescued every day from sin's grip as we walk in the Spirit. This is an ongoing process and is our present, continuous condition until we reach glory, when sin no longer exists because not only will we be in Christ, but we will also be with him for eternity.
3. Glorification—This is our "future complete," a freedom from the presence of sin forevermore. We will finally be free from the Enemy's attacks. We will finally be home—our real home. "For this world is not our permanent home; we are looking forward to a home yet to come" (Hebrews 13:14 NLT).

As we live out our new identity in Christ, we begin to see how we fit into his big picture. We must never to lose sight of this. Our position never changes, but the Enemy wants us to forget this truth, and sometimes we do.

Read Ephesians 2:1–6. We might forget where we left our keys, what we wore last Tuesday, or what we ate for breakfast, but one thing we must remember every day is our position—our true identity.

When we forget our position, we don't live as children of God, we live as children of wrath.

How do we prevent ourselves from forgetting our true identities? Here are some practical ways you can do that.

- Start your day by saying I am a child of God. Proverbs 18:21 says that life and death are in the power of the tongue—speak life-giving words over yourself
- Stay connected with God throughout your day by talking with him
- Memorize Scripture and stand on his promises found in the Bible. Write Scripture on sticky notes and index cards and conspicuously displayed them everywhere
- Surround yourself with godly friends who will pray for and with you and love you through your trials. True friends have your best interests at heart
- Seek wise, godly counsel in times of trouble for direction and encouragement—those who will help you navigate rough seas and break free from toxic relationships

Your Spiritual Birth Certificate

I always wanted my kids to feel special, especially on their birthdays. The night before their birthdays, I'd break out colorful crepe paper and drape it across the dining room ceiling. They'd awake to find a birthday banner hung on the wall and gifts piled high on the table. Every year became a celebration reminding them of the importance of their birth.

We have no doubts about the fact we were born. We have parties, receive gifts, eat cake, and sing the happy birthday song. We even have an official piece of paper to prove it—our birth certificate. We value a piece of paper that tells us when we were born, where we were born, and who our parents are.

The Bible is like our spiritual birth certificate. The Bible tells us how we got here, how to be born again, and who our Father is. We learn more about our true identity in the Bible than from the official document issued by the registrar of the states where we were born.

For instance, the Bible helps you remember (Ephesians 1:3–14):

- You are seated in heavenly places
- You are blessed in the beloved
- You are adopted into the family of God
- You are chosen
- You have an inheritance
- You are forgiven
- You are redeemed through the blood of Jesus
- You are reconciled to the Father through Christ
- You are holy and blameless
- You are sealed with the Holy Spirit

Have you heard what happens when you receive Christ as Savior? A heavenly birthday party. Luke 15:10 says there is rejoicing in the presence of angels when a sinner comes to Christ. The celebration is like a Happy Rebirthday, and worth remembering!

You are a child of God. He lavishes love on you. When you walk in your true position, you can walk in a manner worthy of your calling. You are rooted and established through God's love. When you aren't walking in your place of true position, you are believing a lie about yourself and your identity.

Lies about our identity are false beliefs we infer from our experiences. They come from what:

- People have told us
- We tell ourselves

- People have done to us
- We have done to ourselves
- The Enemy tells us

God's Word dispels lies because the Bible tells the truth of who you are—a beautiful, vibrant branch who grows out from the true vine—Jesus. In Christ, you are justified, are being sanctified day by day, and can look forward to being glorified when you live out eternity with Jesus.

You are a justified, sanctified child of God—that is who you are, and nothing can change that marvelous truth. God created us for his pleasure, or as A.W. Tozer puts it in *The Pursuit of God*, "God made us for Himself."[1]

God desires continued intimacy with us throughout our lives. James 4:8 tells us when we draw near to God, he will draw near to us. In John 15:14–15 he calls us his friends. You, precious daughter of the Most High God, are loved. You and Jesus are BFFs—Jesus and I are BFFs. He never lets us down, never leaves us out, and he never ever forgets our rebirthdays.

Describe your true identity below.

BACK TO THE VINE

What has God revealed to you during this week's study?

LISTEN

Fierce Calling Podcast episode #126
Nicole Jacobsmeyer: "Fighting for Purpose"
https://dorisswift.com/2022/11/29/nicole-jacobsmeyer-fighting-for-a-purpose/

Fierce Calling Podcast episode #107
Lisa Appelo: "God Reshapes What's Shattered So Life Can Be Good Again"
https://dorisswift.com/2022/06/28/lisa-appelo-god-reshapes-whats-shattered-so-life-can-be-good-again/

Fierce Calling Podcast episode #125
Diana Mood: "The Sustaining Power of God's Presence"
https://dorisswift.com/2022/11/22/diana-mood-the-sustaining-power-of-gods-presence/

Fierce Calling Podcast episode #16
Dr. Michelle Bengtson: "God Never Wastes Our Pain: Hope for Your Journey"
https://dorisswift.com/2020/02/18/god-never-wastes-our-pain-hope-for-your-journey-with-dr-michelle-bengtson/

Begin praying now as we head into Week Two, when we surrender the joy stealers revealed and named this week. Pray for the Spirit's leading and what to share with your group. You never know how God will use your story to intersect someone else's to bring healing. Share what he leads you to share. Now is the time to walk free as a child of light.

Are you ready to surrender your joy stealers to God?

WEEK TWO: RESPOND

SURRENDERING YOUR JOY STEALERS

Introduction to Week Two: Surrendering Our Joy Stealers and Releasing Their Grip on Us

Scripture-fed prayer for the journey: Read Psalm 46 and make it a personal prayer

As shades of rose-gold and fiery orange brushed across the horizon, the grandboys gathered dried branches to feed our fire. Those branches, though useful for a time, served a short-lived purpose. Apart from the living tree, their dried-up existence quickly burned to ash. This week, we learn how to surrender our revealed joy stealers and abide in the vine. Learning to abide in Christ and surrender our joy stealers to him releases their grip on us. Now is the time to experience the fullness of joy Jesus promised when he placed his joy in us.

Day One

Surrendering Our Control

Releasing Control to the True Vine

Scripture-fed prayer for the journey: John 15:5

A light rain turned torrential as I drove home from work some years ago. When I approached an intersection, I panicked when the light turned amber, and instead of sailing through it, I hit the brakes. My blue Plymouth Volare skated across the center line—the tire treads no match for the slick pavement. How does that go? Steer into the skid or away from it? The skid happened fast, and as much as I tried, I couldn't gain control. Skidding sideways toward the car on my left, I braced myself for impact. Then something miraculous happened—instead of crashing into that poor sitting-duck, my Volare swerved to the right and missed a collision by a hair. By this time the light was green, but nobody moved—nobody except me, that is. I have no doubt divine intervention carried me through that intersection to the other side without so much as a scratch to my car or anyone else's. Mortified, I continued down the highway hoping the sitting-duck I nearly smashed into wouldn't catch up to me. I thanked the Lord all the way home.

Joy stealers threaten to overtake us, making us swerve in all directions. They tell us to white-knuckle the wheel and try steering our own lives—until things go awry—then they tell us we're the ones out-of-control. Those life-draining events threatening to steal our joy can attempt to derail us like a runaway train—or a car hydroplaning on wet pavement. Here's the good news—Jesus has the answer, and we need not feel out-of-control because control is not our role. It's his.

Jesus establishes our role in John 15. He is the vine, and we are the branches. Isn't that refreshing? As women, we struggle with letting go of control. Can I get an amen? Gripping the wheel of life tightly and trying to control outcomes is a slippery slope—do you know what can start the slide? A slippery slope slide happens when we don't realize we're trying to control everything.

I never considered myself a controlling type. I don't have a take-charge personality. God bless those who do, but I don't. This is what I do have—the desire to make everyone else's lives better. As women, we have been blessed with the gift of nurturing. Not every woman nurtures the same way and that's okay. While nurturing is a positive trait, it can turn into people-pleasing if we're not careful.

I used to be the girl picking up the slack and saying yes before considering whether God wanted me to say yes. Perhaps he wanted me to say no. I confused my people-pleasing ways with serving others, which can be a form of control. What I was doing was controlling my life by putting myself last on every level. I wanted to keep everything under control, peaceful, running smoothly. That can wear a person out. You too? Have you struggled with keeping all the balls in the air and all the plates spinning? Here's a dose of encouragement for you—control is not your job or mine—and it's okay if something crashes to the floor.

Now is the time to surrender, but what does surrendering truly, totally, and completely mean? Do we waive a white flag? Crawl under our beds in defeat? On the contrary, surrender equals victory—not defeat— when our act of surrender is to God.

When you think of the word surrender, what comes to mind?

Surrender might feel like a battle word and rightly so. Here's a definition from the Merriam Webster Dictionary online:

> to yield to the power, control, or possession of another upon compulsion or demand
>
> to give up completely or agree to forgo especially in favor of another
>
> to give [oneself] up into the power of another especially as a prisoner
>
> to give [oneself] over to something (such as an influence)[1]

What does surrender mean for us? We relinquish control, submit to God's will, and surrender all we have and all we are to the Lord. We do this verbally through prayer, and physically through a posture of worship and our actions. Surrendering our joy stealers to God does not mean we're giving up and giving in to them. Surrendering means we're giving up our need to control and accepting God's will for our lives.

Jesus is our example of surrender and submission because he yielded to the Father's will. In Luke 22:42 Jesus said, "… not my will, but yours be done." That powerful prayer to the Father was during the most difficult time in Jesus's earthly life. Fully God, yet fully man, submitting to earthly life from birth to enduring the cross thirty-three years later for all humanity. Amazing love and a beautiful picture of surrender for the good of all mankind.

We are never alone. Once we lean into the Father's will, he helps us accomplish things far beyond what we could do on our own. When we surrender, we're making a divine trade with God—a trade he invites us to as an active participant. We lift our burdens to him in exchange for rest for our souls and peace that surpasses all understanding.

Then, there are those deals we make with God. If God would allow such and such to happen, we promise to do something or stop doing something. God is not interested in making deals. He is interested in the condition of our hearts.

SURRENDERING OUR CHILDREN AND GRANDCHILDREN

Remember the story of my son being put out on his own? I struggled with surrendering him to God even though he belonged to God all along. As a parent, God grants us authority to take control over the lives of the children he entrusts to us, but that's different from surrendering control of our children's lives and choices to God. God is not only our Father, but the Father to our children.

We cannot surrender our own lives without surrendering the lives God has entrusted to us.

The day both our son and daughter sat in the driver's seat about killed me. Granted, they did not do this on the same day, thank God—they were six years apart. Then it happened again with our grandkids. I could rest whenever they drove off only after I got on my knees and surrendered control of their safety and well-being to God. Does that mean they will never experience pain? No. Surrendering means God's will be done in their lives whatever that is—and it might not always be the way we would choose.

I thought of Hannah whenever I felt the urge to take back control over the lives of my kids. We meet Hannah in 1 Samuel.

Read 1 Samuel 1:1–28 (take special note of verses 10 and 11)

Hannah has a surrender story too. Hannah's name means "favor or grace" and we see God's favor and grace upon her.

What strikes you about Hannah's surrender story?

Let's take a moment to read 1 Samuel 2 where we find Hannah's prayer. The Lord also blessed Hannah with three more sons and two daughters. Her firstborn, Samuel, became a prophet through Hannah's full surrender of him to God, but we must consider this was God's plans for him all along. Hannah brought Samuel to Eli to be trained up under godly instruction, but what about her other children? I would imagine she surrendered them to God too while she cared for them at home.

Surrendering our precious kiddos is not easy, and no matter how old they get, we want them to be okay. We can go overboard with overprotection without realizing we might be making it about us. God has entrusted us with precious lives—and raising them in a safe environment is important—but we can relax our grip a little because they belong to him. There comes a time when we need to let go of their choices, even the bad ones, because if they've strayed off the path, they must find their own way back to God. The best thing we can do as moms is pray and trust God with the outcome.

When I interviewed Gina Birkemeier, Licensed Professional Counselor, on my podcast, she asked a question that triggered something within me. Episode 112 was on generational dysfunction and trauma, and she was explaining the fight, flight, freeze, and fawn responses. When she explained the fawn response, she asked, "... do you tend to feel like the people around you need to be okay so that you can be okay?" She wasn't asking me specifically, but this hit me right between the eyes. As women, we are wired to be nurturers, and Gina's question helped me realize something—nurturing isn't the same as fixing. I was trying to be a fixer. Yes, that was me, the diehard fixer-upper, always wanting everyone around me to be okay so I could be okay, but here's the reality:

We can't fix people, but we can fix our eyes on Jesus.

Tethering our hearts to those we love and care about is okay, but nobody ever said we had to tether our hearts to their dysfunction, poor choices, and chaos. We can untether ourselves from the paths they choose, pray for them, love them unconditionally, all while acknowledging we can be okay even if they make choices which we feel are wrong. We can be okay because when we abide in Jesus, we can trust him with the outcome. That is true surrender, and when we do this, we allow the Lord to release everything which hinders us from living our own lives and callings. This is not being uncaring but rather being aware of acceptable boundaries. We have permission to surrender control to God so our lives can get back on track with his plans for us.

Surrendering our children does not mean we have to send them away physically, like Hannah did, but we send away control over our expectations for their lives. We want what's best for them, but so does God and he knows best. God already made plans for them, and as moms, we can pray they will follow Jesus and live out those plans. We might not always agree with their choices—surrendering includes not necessarily accepting their choices but understanding we can't choose for them.

Ironically, Eli the priest, to whom Hannah surrendered the care of Samuel, also had sons. In 1 Samuel 2, we're told Eli's sons were worthless men who didn't know the Lord. And Samuel's sons? They became judges over Israel but accepted bribes and did not uphold justice. However, our children have something their sons didn't have, a Savior who walked in flesh and surrendered his life for them. Whether our kids choose Jesus or not, there is always hope and we can always pray, and we always know God hears us and knows our mamas' hearts.

Our pure surrender touches the merciful and compassionate heart of God.

SURRENDERING OUR MARRIAGES OR OUR SINGLENESS

Perhaps your marriage is struggling and the relationship with your spouse washed downriver long ago. God is with you no matter the condition of a marriage or the outcome. You are the bride of Christ, and although earthly relationships can leave us feeling empty, we are called to empty ourselves so Jesus can fill the echoing caverns of our souls. Surrender your marriage to God and abide in the vine who nourishes his branches. Relationships can be messy is an understatement, amen? Regardless of our past, current, or future relationships, God is able, and everything he allows throughout our lives flows from a place of love. God is love, and his love is perfect even amidst imperfect relationships.

Hannah's story includes a loving husband, but the rival wife, Peninnah, was jealous. As 1 Samuel 1:6 tells us, Peninnah provoked Hannah grievously to irritate her. A culture where there's another wife in the picture is difficult to imagine, but I think some can relate to the relentless badgering from a family member. Marriage isn't always easy, especially when meddling family members are added to the mix. If this is the case for you, God will help you set healthy boundaries to protect your marriage relationship.

In the book introduction, I shared about my speaking engagement at a women's event in 2014. Among the joy stealers scribbled on those slips of paper were stories of broken marriages. I say stories because although there might have only been a few words written, those words represented the enormity of the situation a woman sitting in the room that day was walking through. There were things like feeling disrespected, unloved, husband's drinking problem, addiction, abuse—so much brokenness. God is in the business of mending brokenness. Surrender, prayer, and trusting him with the outcome brings peace and hope.

We have heard we need to put God first in our marriages, but what if a spouse is not willing to do that? The other still can, and prayer changes things.

If you're waiting for a spouse, surrender to God's timing. He already knows who your spouse will be. He created that person with you in mind.

If you're happily single, you and God journey together as you walk in your calling. At times, frustration can envelop you when others equate singleness to loneliness or being incomplete without a spouse. Surrender both meddling and well-meaning friends and family to God. Surrender your heart and God will do the rest.

SURRENDER THE REST OF YOUR FAMILY

There might be family members who consistently threaten to steal your joy. Family brokenness runs deep, and you may find moving forward impossible when family members keep dredging up the problem. You have the right to set boundaries and love others from a distance. Family gatherings might prove challenging, but when someone tries to engage us in a lose-lose debate, we can disengage from the conversation. Just because the Enemy sets a trap doesn't mean we have to set our feet—or our mouths—in his snare.

*To have boundaries while being salt and light
to those walking in darkness is OK.*

Action Step:
Release control of your family and surrender each one by name to God.

SURRENDERING OUR FINANCES

The pain was intense—so intense Brian could barely move. Two trips by ambulance to the emergency room later, the pain was still unbearable, and no medications could touch it. Finally, relief came when he literally crawled on hands and knees into the chiropractor's office. Twice a day for several weeks, we made the trek there until he could finally taper off and feel human again. I'm not suggesting this route for everyone, but it was the right one for Brian and his two ruptured discs. I prayed he would find healing and relief from pain, and praise God he did! Still, as a wife, I wanted desperately to ease his pain. My emotions and his pain weren't the only things draining us, our bank accounts were draining too.

Brian is the sole proprietor of a pest control business he started in 1996. Living in Florida is job security because there is certainly no shortage of bugs here. The flip side is you don't get paid when you are the owner/operator of a business and you don't work. We drained our savings, and our bills fell behind, and although we have every kind of insurance you can imagine, we didn't have the kind that covers missed workdays.

We went through an endless myriad of payment arrangements and payment extensions, which seem helpful at first, but ultimately puts us further behind the eight-ball. Still, I was thankful for all the gracious and compassionate people who helped me work out financial arrangements. I could not control the circumstances, so I surrendered them to the one who holds the future. God gave me favor with our creditors, met our needs, and sustained us through a difficult season.

We easily forget God is our provider when we're in the thick of things. We have his promise, and we can take that to the bank.

Read Philippians 4:19 and write the verse below.

What does this verse mean to you personally?

Now read John 15:5

How does John 15:5 and Philippians 4:19 relate to our needs?

Action Step: Say a prayer surrendering your finances and declaring and thanking God as your source of security.

Surrendering Our Pasts

I'm not proud of some of the things I've done. You too? Here's the great news—God forgives us when we ask for forgiveness. In Mark 1:14–15, Jesus tells us to repent and believe in the gospel. Repentance is an important part of the gospel message, yet our culture would have us believe since God is love, we can leave the repentance part out. Nothing is further from the truth. To repent refers to a change of heart and mind, causing us to turn from old ways toward God's ways. Once we do, we recognize sin and ask forgiveness. Jesus made a way for us to be forgiven through the shedding of his blood on Calvary. There's nothing we've done that can separate us from God's love—he loves us unconditionally. But sin separates us from relationship with God, and our loving God calls us to repent by changing our hearts and minds, believing the gospel of truth, turning from our old ways—to be forgiven and set free.

Read Romans 8:38–39.

Only sin separates us from God, but the blood of Jesus covers our sins and makes us white as snow (as some favorite church hymns remind us). Christ's redemption and forgiveness of sins closed the chasm between sinner and Father.

We can surrender our pasts to God, but what if our past is filled with pain inflicted by the hands of another or many others? There is nobody on earth who can change the past, but there was somebody on earth who came to redeem it. Jesus.

Sometimes, we know exactly which past events hold us back from walking free. Sometimes we don't. When I interviewed friend Billie Jauss on my podcast, she shared how our current struggle can at times be attributed to one specific incident from our past. For example, she struggled with calling herself an author even after two published books. Why? She was able to trace the feeling back to a time when she shared her thoughts on a book assignment, and an English teacher basically told her she didn't know what she was talking about. That was an aha moment. A published author could not see herself as an author—or even a writer—because someone spoke those words over her years before.

Friend, what has someone spoken over you that broke your heart and broke your spirit? What words do you speak over yourself, keeping you back from taking a fresh step forward?

Please read Proverbs 18:21. What does it say?

What does sweet surrender of our thoughts and words look like?

Take a moment to pray about whatever God is calling you to surrender. Your spouse? Your kids? Your grandkids? Your finances? Your past? Your health? You?

So many joy stealers can make life hard, but Jesus said he came that we might not only have life but have abundant life. That doesn't mean life is always easy, but abundant life flows from Jesus even when hard times come.

What does abundant life look like to you?

Surrender is Key to Our Moving Forward

How Do We Surrender?

We start with prayer.

Write a prayer asking God to help you surrender control of your life, loved ones, and outcomes of your circumstances to him.

Now let's write a commitment to God stating we won't take back the control we've surrendered.

Day Two: Surrendering Our Fruitlessness

Releasing Fruitless Lives in Exchange for Fruitful Living

Scripture-fed prayer for the journey: Ephesians 5:8–11

"God can't use me—you don't know where I've been or what I've done." Her words struck a chord in the depths of my heart. They felt familiar, since years before, I had spoken those very words over myself. When we focus on our faults, we limit what God wants to do in our lives. I am reminded of Rahab and Mary Magdalene. Rahab's line of work was prostitution, and Jesus cast seven demons out of Mary Magdalene. God used those women, and he can use us.

> ***God is not interested in our insecurities—
> he's interested in our willingness to go.***

Jesus reconciled us to the Father through his work on the cross. The Father now sees us through his son, and he sees us as the women he created us to be. Let's surrender our insecurities and go where he sends us. John 15 never mentions we must have everything all together to bear much fruit. John 15 also never mentions we must be perfect to bear much fruit.

What does John 15:4 tell us about bearing fruit?

I've wasted hours of my life worrying about whether I was bearing fruit. What is fruit? What does it look like? How do I know if I'm bearing any or if I'll wind up like those burned up, good-for-nothing branches in John 15:6? Maybe you've wondered too. When we use our own fruit-bearing measuring stick, we spend fruitless hours worrying if we measure up to the standard. The truth is, we are already walking a fruit-bearing road when we're following Jesus.

Read Ephesians 5:8–11 and describe below what this verse calls unfruitful.

I live in Florida, and while there aren't many grapevines hanging around where I live, there is an abundance of flowering trees. Crape myrtles line the main highway running through our city, and they're breathtakingly beautiful in full bloom. When they're not blooming? Not so much. The trees are meticulously pruned back in winter, void of color, and nothing about them would take anyone's breath away. Search the internet for images of pruned crape myrtle trees and you'll understand. The trees we see with our physical eyes are fruitless and bare, but the trees we will eventually see are fruitful and abundant—bursts of spectacular blooms for our pleasure. They will never bear grapes, roses, or apples—God gave them a different purpose. We are all capable of bearing much fruit when we abide in the vine—but all our fruit will not be the same. That's the beauty, and our different fruits bring God pleasure. Sometimes our fruit lies dormant, waiting for our next season to bloom.

In her article "How Do Flowers Become Fruit," Elisabeth Ginsburg states, "Every fruit begins with a flower, but not every flower results in a fruit."[2] Isn't that fascinating? We must abide in the vine, because we can't bear fruit without Jesus. If we're not abiding in the vine, it's possible to display a flowering life and still be walking around fruitless. Attending church, joining Bible studies, donating to bake sales are all good things—but are we doing it out of obligation or out of a place of abiding in the vine? Are we doing it to draw attention to ourselves or to honor God?

There's a difference between going through the motions and following through with actions. John 15 tells us the key to bearing fruit.

Read John 15:4–5 and write a synopsis of these two verses.

So often we step out with good intentions but misstep when trying to make things happen on our own. I'm thankful we don't have to produce our own fruit, aren't you? God produces the fruit, and he does that through us when we stay close to him, study his word, converse with him throughout the day, love him with everything we have, love others as ourselves, and go where he sends us. That is abiding, and when we follow through with these actions, we are on the same page with God. When we're in step with God, we avoid missteps in following his plans for us.

Read Ephesians 2:10 provided below.

> For we are his workmanship, created in Christ Jesus for good works, which God prepared beforehand, that we should walk in them.

Paraphrase what this verse tells you.

God gave us talents and abilities we've either nurtured or ignored. The Holy Spirit distributes spiritual gifts to us, and none of us were looking for the restroom when they were handed out. These kingdom assets were never meant for us to keep for ourselves. The world needs our gifts—the world needs your gifts.

Let's surrender what hinders the fruit God wants to produce in and through us. Are you ready to surrender fears, doubts, shame, actions, and everything fruitless in exchange for living a fruitful life?

Write a personal prayer to God below, surrendering all the things hindering your ability to bear much fruit. Surrender to his pruning and ask him to bear much fruit through you. After writing it, pray through it, and I'll see you tomorrow.

Day Three: Surrendering Our Idols

Releasing What We've Placed in God's Place

Scripture-fed prayer for the journey: 1 Corinthians 10:14

I have a confession to make—I envied that perfect family confidently strolling into church on Sunday mornings. Every hair in place as if they just stepped out of a stock photo in one of those picture frames at Walmart. To top that off, the husband was a former professional athlete, so I was sure their home was HGTV picture-perfect too. At the time, my husband wasn't attending church with me, which magnified the issue. I idolized their lives, and I wanted what they had. Wow, during church even! What I didn't know was their lives weren't as perfect as they seemed. Their marriage ended a few years later, and by then, my husband was sitting next to me in church. Instead of idolizing that family, I was now thankful for my own.

Read Exodus 32:1–8

Do you have a golden calf in your backyard? Neither do I, but idols are sneaky. An idol is anything drawing us away from our first love, Jesus. Idols can even be things we'd consider good, like ministry work, but going, going, doing, doing, can become—you guessed it—an idol. Isn't it astonishing how priorities can get so jumbled? Who would think it possible that ministry work could come before God in our lives?

What strikes me about the Exodus passage above is the reason the people urged Aaron to make for them gods, idols—they grew impatient in their waiting. They had no idea what had become of Moses, but instead of trusting the God who walked them to freedom through the Red Sea on dry ground, they chose to create their own version, false gods. We can scoff at them and call them crazy, but here's the crazy part—we do the same thing.

Moses had been on Mount Sinai receiving the Ten Commandments written by the very finger of the one true God. On the thirty-ninth day, the Israelites decided they could wait no longer and needed a golden calf to worship. When did Moses return? On day forty. God sent him back to set them straight.

How many times do we grow impatient in waiting on the Lord? We wait for a dream, an answer to prayer, instructions for our calling, help with finances, diagnoses during a health crisis. So. Much. Waiting. Then we lose patience and turn to idols. We listen to what the world says we should do, where we should go, what we should say. As mentioned earlier, we are notorious for trying to make things happen on our own, and according to our own timelines.

Like when God promised Abram (who later became Abraham) descendants, but several years had passed and his wife Sarai (who later became Sarah), had not conceived. She took matters into her own hands and told her husband Abram to have children with her servant Hagar. We can't blame it all on Sarah. As I recall, Abraham was a willing participant. Those actions of disobedience complicated matters because Hagar's son, Ishmael, was not the son of promise. Isaac, whom Sarah gave birth to about fourteen years later, was. Still, God had mercy on Hagar and Ishmael and through him, a great nation arose.

What draws our attention away from our first love? We do life with others, serve together, perhaps work outside the home, raise our children. There's a healthy balance in all those areas of our lives, and if we're putting God first, we experience a proper alignment. Sometimes, though, we can put other relationships before God and find our lives becoming misaligned.

Surrender the Joy Stealers | 65

Let's surrender our idols to God. If we're unaware of any in our lives, ask the Lord to reveal anything taking the place of God's place. Write a prayer of surrender below and get ready to surrender your thoughts on Day Four.

Day Four: Surrendering Our Thoughts

Releasing the Urge to Dwell on Negative Thoughts

Scripture-fed prayer for the journey: 1 Corinthians 2:16

Our generous church members funded a new playground for families to gather and get to know each other. I have no doubt it will serve the community well and provide hours of playtime fun for years to come. Playgrounds are meant to be enjoyed, but there's an adage that the mind is the devil's playground. This tells us much about what can happen when we allow our thoughts to run amok. However, our minds are not the devil's playgrounds unless we allow him to play there. Why would the devil want to mess with our minds? Our minds are where sin begins. The Enemy can't read our minds, but he can spot our weaknesses a mile away and whisper lies of temptation into our ears. Sinful thoughts will likely lead to sinful actions. That's his game—he wants to incite sinful thoughts so we can be played.

Today's Scripture tells us a different story. As believers, we have the mind of Christ, and when we abide in him, our thoughts are life-giving. When we stray from the vine, our thoughts can wander down treacherous rabbit holes, making up stories that are far from true. Let's be honest, who hasn't thought at least once that if a friend hasn't responded to a text within half an hour or less, she must be mad at us. Right? How about this: If someone doesn't say we did a great job, or they like our new hairstyle, or we look great wearing a new outfit, surely it's because we did a terrible job, our hair is a hot mess, and the outfit looked better on the mannequin. We figure her mother told her if she couldn't say anything nice, she shouldn't say anything at all, so silence equals we don't measure up. Those scenarios might seem shallow, but I can relate. Can you? Our minds are complex, and we can either be intentional thinkers who keep our minds on Christ, or unintentional thinkers who host a playground full of toxic thoughts and downward-spiral thinking. In counseling, we call that "stinking thinking."

Here's the thing about thoughts—we can change them with God's help. Thoughts play a major role in our lives— what we think about God, ourselves, the Bible, others. Thoughts can draw us nearer to God or push us farther away.

Read 2 Corinthians 10:5
What does this verse say about our thoughts?

Now let's back up to 2 Corinthians 10:3-4
What kind of weapons are being used?

What does the word "destroy" refer to in verses 4 and 5?

We're fighting a battle, friend, but we do not fight alone. In fact, the Lord fights for us. Through his divine power, ungodly thoughts can be shut down. Not only do we struggle with our own thoughts daily, but we must diligently resist thoughts coming at us from all sides. False gospels surround us in a world that doesn't understand God's upside-down kingdom. We say upside-down because what Jesus teaches is completely opposite from what culture teaches. We are made in God's image, sanctified day by day to be more and more like Christ. His example on earth was that of humbleness, compassion, and unconditional love—even extending love to enemies. The world doesn't understand loving enemies, and images and messages we see every day can mess with our minds. Thankfully for us, God has provided a strategic plan for us to think right thoughts which lead to right actions.

Read Philippians 4:8 and list what we are to think on below.

Here are practical steps to take thoughts captive.

- Pray Philippians 4:8 and aloud if possible
- Praise God for who he is, what he's done, and his many blessings
- Write Bible verses on index cards and sticky notes
- Sing a favorite worship song
- Serve others

By taking these simple yet profound steps, we honor God, push out unholy thoughts by taking every thought captive, and keep our minds filled with his truth. We can't think evil thoughts when we're praising God or singing a worship song—it's like water displacing air when we fill a glass to quench our thirst. Healthy drinking water is probably filtered. The term "take every thought captive to obey Christ" is a filtering process too. Good thoughts are already under the obedience of Christ and the bad ones, well, bye-bye, you've been displaced. God's truth fosters holy and pure thoughts, and we experience his peace when our minds filter out the bad thoughts.

Read Isaiah 26:3 and write it below.

Why is our mind stayed on him?

When our thoughts are in line with God's truth, it becomes easier and easier to think like Jesus.

Day Five: Surrendering Our Desires

Releasing Our Wants in Exchange for God's Best

Scripture-fed prayer for the journey: Read Psalm 25:4–5 aloud to the Lord

I wanted to be a teacher. When my sister Karen and I attended elementary school, my grandma gifted us with two desks for which we were grateful. Our basement became a schoolroom, and I'd spend hours teaching my dolls and stuffed animals what I had learned at real school. I thought for sure my future was meant for crafting colorful bulletin boards and writing with sticks of white chalk—not the crumbly kind—the smooth kind that snapped when you pressed too hard. My plans were set until a teen pregnancy interrupted them. Or did it? Although I never became a schoolteacher, I taught Sunday School, and later, women's Bible studies. My deep desire for teaching was fulfilled. Not the way I had envisioned, but once I surrendered my dream of teaching to God, he walked me right into his plans for the gift of teaching he gave me.

Do you have unmet desires? Today, we're talking about surrendering our wants for what God knows we need.

Leah's Longing

The story of Jacob, Rachel, and Leah is a messy one—a heartbreaking love triangle—yet fascinating and filled with hope. God didn't leave out any of the sordid details, so we can learn from them. Genesis 29 picks up after Jacob, Isaac's son and Abraham's grandson, fled home at the urging of his mother Rebekah. She knew his brother Esau planned to kill him for two reasons—a stolen birthright and a stolen blessing.

Jacob and Esau were twins, but Esau was the firstborn and first in line to become head of the household. He would also receive a double-portion inheritance from his father's estate. The Bible tells us the trouble began in the womb, where they struggled against each other. Years later, Jacob took advantage of Esau during a weak moment of hunger and talked him into selling his birthright to him for a piece of bread and a bowl of lentil stew. His father, Isaac, was wealthy, and during a moment of weakness, Esau gave up his firstborn birthright. We might snicker over Esau's ridiculous trade, yet how might this apply to our lives? How often have we turned from our first love and toward earthly desires, practically forsaking our birthrights as children of God? I know. I stopped snickering too.

Families are complicated, and just when we think we're the only ones with family drama and generational skeletons lurking in our closets, God's word provides a front-row seat to dysfunction. Jacob was Rebekah's favorite son, so she devised a plan for Jacob to steal Isaac's blessing. A blessing was a type of seal of promise, like a will. Oh, what a tangled web we weave. Hence the Jacob-running-for-his-life thing. His mother sent him off to her brother's place, Jacob's uncle. There Jacob first saw Rachel, his uncle Laban's daughter. She was a shepherdess and caught Jacob's fancy. Yes, evidently, she was his first cousin, but cultural study of that time reveals such marriages were common. At least, they were somewhat certain of the lineage and were keeping it pure. Jacob worked for Laban for seven years to earn the right to marry Rachel. When the seven years passed, a marriage took place—only Jacob didn't marry Rachel—he married her sister Leah. This was a classic bait and switch, as Jacob had no idea that he married the wrong sister until the morning after the wedding night. What a shocker—he was not happy to say the least. Laban purposely deceived Jacob by sending him the wrong daughter. Doesn't that sound familiar? Laban justified his action by stating customarily the firstborn was given in marriage first. Yes, another lesson and biblical concept we can glean from 'you reap what you sow.' Jacob finally married Rachel, but only after he completed the first week of marriage with Leah. When the week was done, Rachel was sent to him but only because he agreed to work another seven years for Laban. The sad thing about all of this? Leah loved Jacob, Jacob loved Rachel, and Leah was unloved. The beauty in all of this? God loved them all.

God saw Leah was unloved by Jacob, and he opened her womb, but Rachel was not yet able to conceive. So not only was Leah unloved by her husband, but her sister also resented her.

Read Genesis 29:31–35

What transformation is taking place within Leah's heart from v. 31 through v. 35?

Leah "ceased bearing" for a time, even offering her servant Zilpah to Jacob, who bore him two sons. Culturally, this was acceptable. It might seem outlandish to us, but in our study of the Bible, we need to understand cultural differences to better understand God's big picture story. This practice was viewed as a sacrifice for the greater good, producing more offspring—more fruit to carry on the lineage.

Read Genesis 30:1–24

Mandrakes were a plant with roots thought to help with fertility, so Leah used them to bargain with Rachel for her night with Jacob. You can't make up this stuff.

Leah dealt with comparison, envy, a seemingly loveless marriage (although Genesis 29:30 says Jacob loved Rachel more, so perhaps he loved Leah in his own way), and a broken relationship with her sister. What Leah experienced would likely cause any girl to feel worthless and void of value. However, Leah's heart knew God, and she knew he saw her. Her desires changed to line up with God's plans for her. We see God's abundant blessings to Leah through her sons. The Levites, who were chosen to serve God in the Temple, were descendants of Leah's through her son Levi.

But the best part of Leah's story? Through Leah's fourth son, Judah, came the tribe of Judah, the Davidic lineage, the lineage of Jesus Christ. Now that's a praise!

> And no one in heaven or on earth or under the earth was able to open the scroll or to look into it, and I began to weep loudly because no one was found worthy to open the scroll or to look into it. And one of the elders said to me, 'Weep no more; behold, the Lion of the tribe of Judah, the Root of David, has conquered, so that he can open the scroll and its seven seals.' Revelation 5:3–5

Leah surrendered the life she wanted for the life she never knew she wanted—to be included as part of the lineage of her Lord and Savior. Surrendering is hard and a daily action of love. If you find yourself taking back things, don't be too hard on yourself. We're all learning and growing together on this journey.

Abiding in the vine is surrendering our trying to do life apart from Jesus. Now that's easy because Jesus loves us, and he is easy to love. His yoke is easy, and his burden is light, just as Matthew 11:30 tells us.

Surrendering our joy stealers and not taking them back doesn't mean our circumstances will instantly change, but a change takes place within our hearts. We release our cares, struggles, and burdens to God and trust him with the outcome. As I type these words, our family is going through a difficult season, which is threatening to steal my joy. My mom's and dad's health diagnoses, family relationships, financial struggles—but one thing is guaranteed, a threat is just that—a threat—and even amidst heartache and hardship, my joy remains full. These hardships and heartaches of life can feel like black clouds overhead, amen? The good news is the Son always shines through. I believe living through these hard seasons while writing this study is God showing me he is near, and he's near to you too. Joy, hardships, and heartaches *can* and *do* exist simultaneously throughout our lives. We might feel as though difficult seasons overshadow our joy, but whatever we're feeling, we can be sure our joy remains constant. Pain might lessen or it might not. There might be craters in our hearts where that person used to be or where that dream died. This doesn't mean our joy isn't full—it just means we need more of Jesus and to continually abide in the vine.

Last week, we revealed our joy stealers, and this week, we responded. We surrendered our control, our fruitlessness, our idols, our thoughts, and our desires to God. Most importantly, we surrendered our hearts to him.

BACK TO THE VINE

What has God revealed to you during this week's study?

LISTEN

Fierce Calling Podcast episode #119

Michelle Lazurek: "When Struggles Teach Us What It Means to Surrender All"

https://dorisswift.com/2022/09/20/michelle-lazurek-when-struggles-teach-us-what-it-means-to-surrender-all/

Fierce Calling Podcast episode #112

Gina Birkemeier: "Breaking Free from Generational Dysfunction and Trauma"

https://dorisswift.com/2022/08/02/gina-birkemeier-breaking-free-from-generational-dysfunction-and-trauma/

Fierce Calling Podcast episode #110

Billie Jauss: "Detoxing from Internal Distractions & Emotional Toxins"

https://dorisswift.com/2022/07/19/billie-jauss-detoxing-from-internal-distractions-emotional-toxins/

WEEK THREE: RECEIVE

Introduction: Receiving Joy and Abiding in the Vine

Scripture-fed prayer for the journey: Read John 15:1–8 and make it a personal prayer

What do the words "receive" and "abide" mean to you? In Acts 20:35, the Apostle Paul quotes Jesus as saying, "It is more blessed to give than to receive." Jesus taught us to give generously and unselfishly, especially to those in need. As givers, we sometimes find it hard to receive, amen? But Jesus calls us not only to give, but also to receive what he freely gives to us.

How about abide? Does abiding remind you of parental rules, acting in accordance with the law, or something we must endure? I used to associate abiding with those references as well but to abide means so much more.

Today we're exploring these concepts and connecting the dots between receiving, abiding, and how they relate to abundant joy.

Day One: Receiving His Call to Bear Much Fruit

Abiding in the Vine and Why We Need Pruning

Scripture-fed prayer for the journey: John 15:2

Do you struggle with posture? When my daughter was a preteen and regular passenger in my backseat, she used to catch me slouching while driving. We agreed each time she noticed my imperfect posture, her cue would be, "You're doing it!" and I'd immediately sit straight. Believe me, she was good at her job.

Can you believe I still need to remind myself of this? To give you a clue how long I've been working on this, my daughter is now in her thirties. I'm not sure why I have such difficulty sitting and standing straight. Perhaps slouching is more comfortable, but it isn't pretty. Good posture is important for physical health, but when we're talking about abiding in the vine, posture goes much deeper than walking with a book on our heads. Abiding is a conscious behavior of standing firm, walking humbly, and maintaining a posture of praise to the Lord in all we do. Yet there are times when we need pruning, like my daughter reminding me to straighten up. Pruning might look like letting go of an unhealthy relationship, giving up a habit, or changing the direction of the path we're currently on. Pruning might not feel all warm and fuzzy, but according to John 15:2, pruning is a necessary process for bearing more fruit. We want to be pruned and the incredible thing about this pruning process? It is intricately and intimately done by the Father's hand.

Read John 15:2 and write it below.

I learned long ago that vinedressers tenderly prune their vineyard by hand. They must get their hands deep within the thick of the branches to cut back what hinders growth. Grapes can still grow on unpruned vines, but eventually, overgrowth chokes out the once fruitful vine, and it will be rendered useless. Overgrowth also blocks needed light from the sun.

> If anyone does not abide in me he is thrown away like a branch and withers; and the branches are gathered, thrown into the fire, and burned. (John 15:6)

This verse can be a bit unsettling, amen? But fear not, abiding in Jesus, our true vine, will keep us from being thrown into the fire and burned to ashes. Isn't it a sad thought, missing our calling and our futures packed with potential? We'd miss every blessing of being used by God and partnering with him in kingdom work. Sister, this is not you, and this is not me. God has plans for us, and he's told us so (see Jeremiah 29:11). Invite his pruning and surrender whatever he wants to cut back from your life.

In the Old Testament, Israel was referred to as a vine planted by God. Isaiah 5:1-7 paints a picture of how sinful disobedience among his people produced wild grapes rather than a healthy, abundant harvest of good fruit. Sin always leads to consequences, but take heart! A divine rescue was on the way for all of humanity. Through God's amazing plan of salvation, Jesus came as the true vine. As John 15:5 says, apart from Jesus we can do nothing. The word "do" is key here, because what does Ephesians 2:10 tell us about doing?

Write the verse below and answer these investigative questions.

Who?

What?

Where?

When?

How?

See John 15:7–8 below:

> If you abide in me, and my words abide in you, ask whatever you wish, and it will be done for you. By this my Father is glorified, that you bear much fruit and so prove to be my disciples.

As you read those verses, his words are abiding in you. Ask the Father to prune according to his will and plans for your life. Bearing much fruit follows, and in this, our Father is glorified.

What is the evidence of being a disciple of Christ?

Here is a powerful quote by D.A. Carson:

> In short, Christians must remember that the fruit that issues out of their obedient faith-union with Christ lies at the heart of how Jesus brings glory to his Father. Those who are contemplating the claims of the gospel, like John's readers, must reckon with the fact that failure to honour the Son is failure to honour God (5:23). Fruitlessness not only threatens fire (v. 6) but robs God of the glory rightly his.[1]

Write a personal prayer below, surrendering to God those things he desires to prune away, and asking that he blooms much fruit through you.

Day Two: Receiving His Call to Discipleship

Abiding in Him and How His Words Abide in Us

I was a banker for twenty-nine years. I began my career in April 1981, and since it was spring, I guess you could have called me a spring chicken. I had no clue about banking or running a teller drawer. However, I did know a thing or two about money. I didn't have any. What better job for a woman like me not only to earn money, but also to be accountable for it?

Every good teller knows the goal set before us—achieving the perfect balance between what you take in and what you give out. I was trained for the job, became proficient, then trained others. As the years went by, my positions at the bank changed, but I still trained others who were just a few steps behind me. The best part of the job wasn't about the money, but about the people we served. As believers, we want to strike a balance between what we take in from God's word, and what we give out to others in love and service.

Read Hebrews 12:1

Circle where you see "let us" mentioned. If you'd rather not mark your Bible, write those words within the margin of your study book, twice. God never meant us to run this race alone. We continue together on mission, walking in faith as the Old Testament heroes did (see Hebrews 11). Although they suffered much for the faith, Hebrews 11:40 reminds they did not receive what was promised—the Messiah. The verse states, "God had provided something better for us" and through Christ, we were all made perfect together.

In banking and in life, one thing is certain—you never throw a newbie out on their own without training. So how did this training work in banking?

Newbies were required to:

- Read the training manual
- Observe a seasoned worker
- Work alongside a seasoned worker
- Work while a seasoned worker observed and coached you
- Become a seasoned worker through continual learning and doing
- Be the seasoned worker who trains the newbie

There's a pattern here which we can apply to the disciple-making process. Plus, while a trainee sees us doing things well, they also see us doing things not so well. They'll learn more by observing how we handle the not so well stuff, because, let's be real, anyone can handle the well stuff.

We don't have to be perfect at it—just willing. If you feel ill-equipped to disciple someone, I'm sure God has already been equipping you for years. Even if you've never trained someone in a work environment, you've likely taught younger siblings or someone else to cook, read, or even mow a lawn—there is an art to that according to my husband and dad. If you've accepted Jesus as your Lord and Savior, you've been reading your Bible for a while, you have the makings of a disciple-maker.

You've probably realized our training manual is the Bible. God's word, God breathed. Here you go.

> All Scripture is breathed out by God and profitable for teaching, for reproof, for correction, and for training in righteousness, that the man of God may be complete, equipped for every good work. (2 Timothy 3:16–17)

We wouldn't expect an infant to drive a car, right? I know some of you younger mamas have no doubt your infant child is a genius, but even if they could read the manual, they still couldn't reach the pedals. Discipleship is helping others grow until they can reach the pedals. Then they too can drive discipleship. Discipleship is all about being like the feet-washing, teaching, training, praying Jesus. He founded the program. He could have done it all himself, but he didn't. That's where we come in.

Here's some discipleship driving tips.

- Discipleship is not only telling others to study the manual, but studying it with them, and showing them how to apply it.
- Discipleship is not about being perfect, but about being real. How do we deal with the real?
- Discipleship is about relationship, determination, and communication
- Discipleship is observing me so you will know, then I'll help you, so we both grow
- Discipleship is sowing seeds into someone's life, then allowing the Holy Spirit to create the blooms
- Discipleship is finding a balance between what we take in and what we give out
- Discipleship is how we drive the gospel, and we can't lose sight of that
- Discipleship begins with relationship.

This all sounds great, right? But are you wondering where to start? Discipleship is all about God's grace, the story of how we met Jesus, and how he transformed our lives.

Grace—Our Story—Our Grace Story

Leading others to Christ begins by building relationships. Building relationships goes beyond waiving at our next-door neighbor—it's a willingness to invite others into our lives. We get to know them, and they get to see what following Jesus looks like. I don't mean invite them to move in, but rather invite them to lean into our lives and ultimately, Jesus. Building relationships is not about hidden agendas to save people. Only Jesus saves. When our hearts are in the right place, we love others like Jesus loves them and pray for changed hearts. We were created to crave relationships. Sharing about our most precious relationship—with Jesus—is all we need to do. There are times an invitation to follow Jesus comes by way of altar call or praying for someone on the street— but often, the invitation comes by allowing others, as the Spirit leads us, to gain access to our lives. They'll see what we're made of when things get tough. We're made of Jesus in us, the hope of glory. We have peace surpassing all understanding and enough hope for today plus all our tomorrows. This supernatural, genuine peace overflows amid life's storms. People will see our authenticity, hope, peace, and joy. They'll want what we have too because the world isn't offering what Jesus offers them. All this doesn't mean we live perfect lives, but rather lives saturated with perfect love—God's love.

Share your grace story with others so they can be inspired to share theirs. Pray for opportunities to disciple and witness to others because God has the plans, and we are the beautiful feet that bring the good news. Yes, God says our feet are beautiful because they take us where he sends us (see Romans 10:15). God might lead you to a peer, or he may be calling you to sow into the next generation.

An important thing to remember is newbies to the faith aren't the only ones in need of discipling. Many Christians who accepted Christ years ago have never been discipled. Perhaps that's you, and that's okay. There's no shame in seeking a spiritual mentor, so don't allow others to make you feel that way. What way? Like you should have known the ropes by now, discipled your entire neighborhood by now, have this Christianity thing down pat by now—no. None of us are perfect at living a Christian life, but the best news besides the good news? We don't live a godly life alone because the Holy Spirit empowers us. Find yourself a good disciple-maker. You probably already know one.

Write a prayer below asking God to help you abide in his word, and who you might disciple or who might disciple you.

Day Three: Receiving His Call to Joy So that Our Joy May Be Full

Abiding in His Love and Keeping His Commandments

Scripture-fed prayer for the journey: John 15:10–11

Living was difficult as wilderness wanderers, and the Israelites had a hard time keeping God's commandments. They rejoiced in their freedom from slavery, but when the going got tough, they were ready to run back to their previous bondage. We can struggle with a wilderness mentality too. When life gets hard, we are tempted to run back to what's familiar. The only thing is, some of those familiar things kept us bound. We seek to be comforted, which is a normal and natural response to trauma and pain.

Jesus makes us new. He poured himself out so we could be free of the chains that dug into our wrists for way too long. In Christ, we are a new creation—transformed, redeemed. Running back to our old selves is not an option. Here's some encouragement for you today.

> **We cannot run back to our old selves—only our old ways—but Jesus made a new way for us.**

Let's look together at John 15:9–11.

How many times is the word "love" used throughout these verses?

Whose love are these verses referring to?

Personal reflection: How does this love pertain to me?

What does Jesus tell us is key to abiding in his love?

Read Matthew 22:34–40 and write below the commandments Jesus mentions:

We can clearly see how love is an integral part of our existence because the one who formed our existence is love. God is love, and he made us in his image. Through this divine love—*agapē* love—we have a deep desire to keep the commandments Jesus gave us. By his grace and through his love, we abide in Jesus, the true vine, and through our intimate relationship with the true vine, his joy flows through us so our joy can be full.

And what exactly is the joy Jesus speaks of?

Turn to Hebrews 12:2. What brought Jesus joy?

Joy is divine, and isn't that divine? We do not determine what joy is because Jesus gives us the definition. We can say we feel happy—happy about a milestone, an event, when things go our way—but joy is a different story. Our Creator created joy, and our joy is rooted in Christ and receiving the ministry of reconciliation. What is our greatest joy above all and the most meaningful experience of the joy we have?

Read 2 Corinthians 5:11–21 and create a mini-journal entry below of what this means to you and for you.

DAY FOUR: RECEIVING HIS CALL TO FRIENDSHIP

ABIDING IN RELATIONSHIP WITH HIM AND WALKING IN OUR CALLING

Scripture-fed prayer for the journey: Ephesians 4:1

On the day after Christmas 1970, eight-year-old me invited a friend over for cookies and hot chocolate. This was the friend with the cool pool-party house, a phone and TV in her room, and a closet full of the latest fashions. You might have had a friend like her too. I wasn't lacking anything, but as I surveyed the gifts under the tree, I felt there wasn't enough stuff to impress my friend. Isn't that crazy? At eight years old, I had already fallen into the comparison trap. So, what did I do? I fluffed my stuff. I went digging through my closet, pulling dresses, pants, shirts, and tucked them snuggly into boxes lined with white tissue paper. I placed them around the tree, fluffing the stuff already there. The irony was my friend didn't seem the least bit impressed! I felt like saying, "Excuse me, do you know all the trouble I went to just to impress you?" Of course, I didn't, but I sure wanted to! I never forgot the ridiculous lengths I went to, not only to impress a friend, but to make myself feel worthy. What kind of friendship foundation was I building? My friend was my friend which should have been enough—my own insecurities tainted something beautiful.

I finally realized true friendships are built on authentic relationships. No friendship is perfect, but true friendship never includes fluffing our stuff. Friends come and go throughout our lives, but special friendships last over a lifetime—friends who we can call or text at any hour. Are we that friend to someone too? I've also learned God places people in our lives according to his will and timing.

Some relationships are meant to last years and some for just a season. He has good reasons for his timing, and we'll never know the boundaries he has set for our good.

We find the true meaning of friendship here.

> This is my commandment, that you love one another as I have loved you. Greater love has no one than this, that someone lay down his life for his friends. You are my friends if you do what I command you. No longer do I call you servants, for the servant does not know what his master is doing; but I have called you friends, for all that I have heard from my Father I have made known to you. You did not choose me, but I chose you and appointed you that you should go and bear fruit and that your fruit should abide, so that whatever you ask the Father in my name, he may give it to you. These things I command you, so that you will love one another. (John 15:12–17)

What does it mean to you that Jesus calls you friend?

What do we glean from this passage regarding what true friendship looks like? (Take time to dig deep here)

What does Jesus say about fruit and how does fruit connect to friendship with him?

Spend time sitting in a quiet space, pondering the meaning of true friendship and how Jesus calls you friend. Write any reflective thoughts on the next page.

Day Five: Receiving His Call of Empowerment Through the Spirit of Truth

Abiding in the Holy Spirit and Listening for His Guidance

Scripture-fed prayer for the journey: Acts 1:8

When I was ten, my superpower of choice was invisibility. I remember pulling a chair up to the kitchen window, raising the wood frame high enough to allow the crisp night air to seep in, and imagining what it would be like to step out into the night. Since I was invisible, I could walk anywhere without being detected. I'd trek around spying on friends and nosing around where I had no business being (I was ten, remember).

While being invisible would be amazing, we have something more amazing than a superpower. We have the supernatural power of the Holy Spirit who indwells us. The same power that resurrected Jesus lives in us. Sometimes, we forget that extraordinary fact. We forget because life is hard, and when the weight of our circumstances sits squarely on our chests, we try walking by our own strength. We feel powerless because self-made power will fail us every time. We forget we have access to power far beyond human limitations. In 2 Corinthians 12:9, Paul shares these powerful words spoken to him by Jesus: " 'My grace is sufficient for you, for my power is made perfect in weakness.' Therefore I will boast all the more gladly about my weaknesses, so that Christ's power may rest on me.' "

Growing up, I was taught about the Holy Spirit's existence. However, the Holy Spirit remained a mystery to me when I heard stories about the Father talking with Moses through a burning bush and Jesus feeding five thousand people with a loaf of bread and a handful of fish. The more I learned about the Holy Spirit, the more my desire grew to know him in a deeper, more personal way. I wanted to understand why he was sent to indwell us, and what being empowered by him means. I felt compelled to help others know him too.

WHO IS THE HOLY SPIRIT?

Genesis 1:2 tells us the Spirit of God hovered over the earth at creation. In the Old Testament before Jesus came to earth, the Holy Spirt moved on people to empower their purpose. He was poured out on them, indwelled them, and empowered them for a mission, but on a God-assigned, as-needed basis. The men and women of the Bible were called and empowered as we are, yet our access to the Holy Spirit today is much more personal because it's permanent. We can have an amazing relationship with the one who indwells us. How amazing that he knows us and wants us to know him.

According to Scripture, the Holy Spirit is God the Holy Spirit. Although the term "trinity" is not found in Scripture, the triune God—one God in three persons, is.

We see this in Hebrews 10:15–18.

> And the Holy Spirit also bears witness to us; for after saying, 'This is the covenant that I will make with them after those days, declares the Lord: I will put my laws on their hearts, and write them on their minds,' then he adds, 'I will remember their sins and their lawless deeds no more.' Where there is forgiveness of these, there is no longer any offering for sin.

In Acts 28:25–28, Paul quotes the Holy Spirit's words spoken through the prophet Isaiah. Another great example of this in Scripture is found in Acts 4. Here the Bible talks about how believers pooled their money together to be distributed among them. Every need was met because everyone sold their property and turned all the proceeds over to the apostles. Well, almost everyone.

Ananias and Sapphira, a husband and wife, sold a piece of property then decided to keep back a portion from the sale. Ananias brought the rest of the money to the apostles but lied about the sale price. As Ananias laid the proceeds at the apostles' feet, Peter asks him in Acts 5:3 how was it that Satan so filled his heart that he would lie to the Holy Spirit? Then in Acts 5:4, Peter tells Ananias he didn't just lie to humans but to God. When Ananias heard those words, he fell to the ground and breathed his last breath. Then Sapphira arrived on the scene about three hours later, told the same lie, and faced the same fate. Peter first states the Holy Spirit was lied to, then in the same conversation and speaking of the same Person, he states God was lied to. Ananias and Sapphira both lied to God the Holy Spirit.

The Holy Spirit has the attributes all three persons of the Godhead share, such as omnipotence—having almighty power (Isaiah 40:12–14); omnipresence—being ever-present everywhere (Psalm 139:7); omniscience—all knowing (1 Corinthians 2:10–11).

What else do we know about the Holy Spirit? He is the Spirit of wisdom, understanding, and knowledge (Exodus 31:3). He is the Spirit of grace (Hebrews 10:29) and reveals truth. He has a will, and 1 Corinthians 2:10–11 tells us he searches the deep things of God and is the only one who knows the thoughts of God—and he tells us the Father's will (John 16:13).

The Holy Spirit is a person who teaches, guides, speaks to, and intercedes for us. The Bible tells us the Holy Spirit has emotions too. In Isaiah 63:10, we learn the rebellious people grieved the Holy Spirit. Why? Because he loved them. Romans 8:26 assures us that when we do not know how to pray, the Spirit himself intercedes for us with groanings too deep for words. The Holy Spirit is emotional. Doesn't that just warm your heart? Mine too.

What Does the Holy Spirit Look Like?

The Holy Spirit was revealed in different forms. He descended as a dove after Jesus was baptized. In John 3:8, Jesus describes the Spirit to Nicodemus as being like the wind. According to *Strong's Concordance*,[2] the Greek word for wind in that verse is *pneuma*, which refers to both wind and Spirit. In John 7:37–39, Jesus describes the Holy Spirit as rivers of living water to quench our thirst and flow within us.

The Holy Spirit has been described in many ways throughout the Bible. While all these descriptions are fascinating, the most exciting news for believers is the Holy Spirit indwells us—permanently.

Why and Where Does the Holy Spirit Indwell Us?

After Jesus ascended into heaven, a sacred day—referred to as the Day of Pentecost—changed the lives of Jesus followers forever. On that day, believers received the permanent indwelling of the Holy Spirit.

Before Jesus, our High Priest, came as a sacrifice for all, only an appointed high priest in Bible times could offer a sacrifice for his own sin and the sin of the people of Israel. The high priest would enter the Holy of Holies, a sacred room located in the innermost place of the tabernacle and later, the temple, where God would appear once a year. A heavy drape known as the veil separated the Holy of Holies from the rest of the temple—a barrier between God and us. This barrier represented our sin because sin separates us from God. The veil was torn when Jesus died for our sins. No longer was there a separation between God and us because Jesus broke that barrier. Through him we can reach the Father.

When Jesus left the earth he sent the Comforter—the Holy Spirit—to indwell us. No longer was the Holy of Holies located inside the temple needed, because now, our bodies house the Spirit of the Lord—we are his temples. A reminder of this is when Paul asks a poignant question in 1 Corinthians 3:16.

What does Paul ask?

Wrapping our brains around what indwelling of the Holy Spirit means is difficult, yet Jesus himself makes this truth known to us.

> And I will ask the Father, and he will give you another Helper, to be with you forever, even the Spirit of truth, whom the world cannot receive, because it neither sees him nor knows him. You know him, for he dwells with you and will be in you. (John 14:16–17)

Circle the names Jesus gives the Holy Spirit in the verses above.

God understands how hard his higher ways are for us to understand. The Spirit himself inspired Paul to write and remind us again in 1 Corinthians 6:19 that we are the temple of the Holy Spirit, and he is in us. But where in us? Our arms, our legs, our hearts? We want to assign a physical place because physical places are familiar to us. During a sermon a few years ago, one of our pastors, David Lane, explained the indwelling of the Holy Spirit does not refer to a spatial place but rather a transformation by grace. When the Holy Spirit indwells us, we become a temple, the new Holy of Holies housing the presence of God.

You Are Sealed by the Spirit

I love using plastic food containers for leftovers. I believe you can relate to the part I don't love—finding the matching lid. I either can't find any lids or find ten of the wrong size—using the wrong size just won't do the trick. The matching lid is essential to the design. The correct lid creates a seal, locking in freshness and protecting the contents from outside elements. When I take them to a potluck or to work, I mark the lid with my initials because we can never remember which ones belong to us.

When we are in Christ, we too are sealed, and there is no mistaking we belong to him. Read Ephesians 1:13

What have we been sealed with?

Throughout history, a seal represented someone of authority granting approval or making a declaration on an important document. An engraved stamp, bearing the unique design of its owner, created a seal upon impact with a softer material such as colored wax or clay. The seal authenticated the document, validating its worth. We too are sealed upon impact. The moment we believed, the Holy Spirit sealed us, and God authenticated and validated us as his own. Our worth isn't found in our work, our possessions, our education, our appearance, being good enough, thin enough, smart enough, pretty enough, or any other worldly definition of worthiness. Our worth is found in who we belong to, and we belong to Christ.

A seal authenticates and validates ownership, but also protects. When you walk into a bank, it's hard to miss the 5,000-pound steel vault door. That vault door stays open during the day, allowing customers to access safety deposit boxes where they store their valuables. When the bank closes, customers trust bank employees to seal off the vault, keeping intruders out and their valuables safe. We, as believers, have been sealed by the Holy Spirit, a seal that cannot be broken—our treasured faith is secured. We are his and he is ours—he indwells and empowers us to share the gospel and do what God calls us to do.

YOU ARE EMPOWERED BY THE SPIRIT

Florida, where I live, is known as the Sunshine State. Beautiful beaches, tropical weather, and no shortage of outdoor activities just outside our front doors. However, there's another side to Florida we don't like talking about. Hurricane season. We know a storm is brewing when the Weather Channel peeps show up. That's never a good sign.

Floridians might joke about hurricane parties—they're popular down here—but we can't underestimate the power and fury of these destructive storms. No matter the strength rated by category, we almost always lose power. Sometimes for days. When the generator runs out of gas, all power is gone.

Here's the good news—we have access to a power that doesn't need gas, a generator, or a power company. We have access to Holy Spirit empowerment. Evidence of the Spirit's presence in us is displayed outwardly by our fruit. When the Father sent the Spirit to that upper room to the waiting, willing believers, the Spirit made his arrival known in a powerful way.

When Jesus instructed his followers to gather in the upper room and wait, they had no idea what they were waiting for. Acts 2:2 uses the term "suddenly" as the verse describes the arrival of a mighty rushing wind that filled the entire place where they were gathered.

Throughout the Bible, we read accounts of ordinary people doing extraordinary things when emboldened by the Holy Spirit. Think about it. How could regular people tear a lion with bare hands, slay a giant with a sling and a stone, save a nation, walk on water, cast out demons, help the lame to walk, the blind to see, and the dead to rise—and how does a virgin give birth to a Son? The answer: by the power of the Spirit of the living God—the same Spirit who lives in us.

Our callings won't always feel safe, like serving at Vacation Bible School or decorating the church for Christmas does. At times, a calling will feel risky, like going where Christians are persecuted or into dark seedy places. All the things we're called to do are purposeful for the kingdom, but some might call for more boldness. Evil is real and the powers of darkness are closer than we'd like to think. That is why we need the empowerment of the Holy Spirit. We are not overcome by evil but can overcome evil with good (see Romans 12:21).

Women empowered by the Holy Spirit are productive—not destructive like hurricanes or even who we were before we met Jesus. The supernatural power of the Holy Spirit empowers us to accomplish what we could never do on our own. Only with his help can we do what he calls us to do. He is the Helper who advocates for us, comforts us, teaches us, and empowers us in our calling.

Here are some ways the Holy Spirit comforts, equips and empowers us.

- He draws us to salvation through his God-breathed Word (2 Thessalonians 2:14)
- He teaches us all things (1 Corinthians 2:13)
- He helps us remember all Jesus taught (John 14:26)
- He guides us in all truth (John 16:13)
- He calls us to be set apart for the work he calls us to do (Acts 13:2)
- He leads us where to go and where not to go (Acts 11:12; Acts 16:7)

- He gives us life (John 6:63; Romans 8:11; Matthew 1:18)
- He testifies with our spirit that we are children of God (Romans 8:16)
- He looks out for our best interests (Acts 15:28)
- He is with us forever and never leaves (John 14:16)
- He reveals things to come (Luke 2:25–26)
- He renews us (Titus 3:5)
- He brings joy (1 Thessalonians 1:6)
- He fills us with power (Micah 3:8)
- He gives us understanding of the Bible—The Sword of the Spirit (2 Peter 1:21; Ephesians 6:17)
- He intercedes in our weakness when we don't know how to pray (Romans 8:26)
- He brings us hope by his power (Romans 15:13)
- He convicts us of sin (John 16:8–14)
- He sanctifies us (2 Thessalonians 2:13)
- He provides what we need (Philippians 1:19)
- He imparts knowledge of the things of God (1 Corinthians 2:12)
- He speaks for us and through us (Matthew 10:20)
- He gives us liberty (2 Corinthians 3:17)
- He distributes spiritual gifts to us (1 Corinthians 12:4-11)
- He fellowships with us (2 Corinthians 13:14)
- He loves us, for God is love (1 John 4:8)

The Holy Spirit is God the Spirit. These verses help us learn more about his attributes and character, but who he is cannot be confined to a list. How is it possible for Christians to forget the Spirit of God is with us? We forget to ask our Helper for help when our bodies are weary and our minds are spinning. He is ready and waiting for us to connect with him and acknowledge his presence in our lives. We are sealed, and we are loved.

Evidence of the Holy Spirit in You

The Spirit will anoint you and equip you in your fierce calling. You are chosen, set apart, sanctified. Second Corinthians 1:21–22 tells us, "And it is God who establishes us with you in Christ, and has anointed us, and who has also put his seal on us and given us his Spirit in our hearts as a guarantee."

God has chosen you. He prepares you for divine appointments he's already added to your spiritual calendar. If you don't feel ready, that's okay because he equips us as we go—like on-the-job training. Don't hesitate to take action when you feel him prompting you. The Spirit in you will lead the way so others can see your Jesus light shining through. His presence in you will open doors to places that would otherwise be inaccessible. He'll give you favor with people who would otherwise be unapproachable. His work in and through you will be undeniable to those seeking hope. You have the message of hope they need to hear.

Evidence of the Spirit in you is also displayed through the fruit of the Spirit. We'll talk more about that during Week Four.

Ask for the Spirit's Help with Confidence

I met one of my former bank customers at a nail salon a few months ago. I knew this lovely lady well, having served her for many years. The problem was I couldn't think of her name to save my life. We greeted each other with a warm hug and a "Hi, how are you?" but I desperately wanted to call her by name.

Using a person's name makes people feel known and special. I talk to God when I can't rely on my brain cells to awaken. Not aloud of course. I didn't want anyone thinking

I'd inhaled too much nail polish remover. I just spoke to the Lord and asked him to please help me remember her name. Within moments, her name came to me.

In John 14:26, Jesus tells us the Spirit is our Advocate, our Helper, and he will teach us all things and to help us remember—so I asked for his help, and he answered. He helps us in many other ways as well. Through revelation knowledge, he helps us understand what we read in the Bible. After all, he inspired men to write the Bible (2 Timothy 3:16–17).

He also helps us apply God's truth to our lives. We, friend, are the continuing book of Acts. On those days when you don't feel particularly ready to act, the Spirit can lift your spirit through his living water refreshment deep within your soul as Jesus said in John 7:38–39. Drink it up and be assured, the Spirit empowers you to do what God calls you to do. All you need to be is willing and obedient to the call of God on your life.

WALK BY THE SPIRIT ONE STEP AT A TIME

Paul writes to the Galatians, "But I say, walk by the Spirit, and you will not gratify the desires of the flesh. For the desires of the flesh are against the Spirit, and the desires of the Spirit are against the flesh, for these are opposed to each other, to keep you from doing the things you want to do" (Galatians 5:16–17).

BACK TO THE VINE

Read John 15:26–27
Who sent the Holy Spirit and whom was he sent from?

We are in community and relationship with the Father, Son, and Holy Spirit. How awesome is that? Awestruck wonder too beautiful for words. You are a daughter of the King. Walk boldly in the empowerment you already have. The Holy Spirit will help you as you are sanctified day by day, set apart for your purpose and calling. Talk with Him every day throughout the day. We were created for relationship with the Father, Son, and Holy Spirit. I once heard trusted writing coach and mentor, Chad R. Allen, talk about how living a more abundant life happens when we experience healthy relationships.

Connecting with the Spirit is an amazing relationship God gave us as a gift. Never doubt we have been called and chosen. Whenever we feel those doubts creeping in—whenever we wonder if the words Jesus spoke were directed to his disciples and not to us—we need to return to this verse:

> As you sent me into the world, so I have sent them into the world. And for their sake I consecrate myself, that they also may be sanctified in truth. I do not ask for these only, but also for those who will believe in me through their word, that they may all be one, just as you, Father, are in me, and I in you, that they also may be in us, so that the world may believe that you have sent me. (John 17:18–21)

We can believe that truth with all our hearts, receive God's truth with joy, and thank God for his truth every day. Jesus prays to the Father not just for his disciples but for those who will believe in him through their word—that's us, friend. Jesus prays for us and what could be sweeter?

What has God revealed to you during this week's study?

LISTEN

Fierce Calling Podcast episode #39
Suzie Eller: "The Power of Living a Life Marked by Joy"
https://dorisswift.com/2020/07/28/39-the-power-of-living-a-life-marked-by-joy-with-guest-suzie-eller/

Fierce Calling Podcast episode #97
Linda Evans Shepherd: "Transformative Prayer Experiences with God"
https://dorisswift.com/2022/04/19/linda-evans-shepherd-transformative-prayer-experiences-with-god/

Fierce Calling Podcast episode #72
Yvette Walker: "Experiencing the Joy of Hearing from God"
https://dorisswift.com/2021/10/19/yvette-walker/

WEEK FOUR: RENEW

AWAKENING TO THE JOY JESUS GAVE US

Introduction: Renewing Our All and Awakening to the Jesus Joy We Have

Scripture-fed prayer for the journey: Read Isaiah 40 and make verse 40:31 a personal prayer

When I was around seven years old, I told my dad about a bad dream I'd had the night before. Scared me silly. Dad told me next time I had one of those scared-silly dreams, I should stare down the scary and say, "You're not real. This is a dream, and I'm going to open my eyes now," then force my eyes open. That night—the dream returned—except this time I was armed for the battle. I said those words Dad told me to say and forced myself awake. You know what? My dad's advice worked.

Day One: Renewing Our Strength Awakens Our Joy

AWAKENING TO A DEEPER LEVEL OF HOPE AND TRUST IN GOD

Scripture-fed prayer for the journey: Isaiah 40:31

What comes to mind when you hear the word strength? Old-school me would say the image of Popeye the Sailor Man opening a can of spinach, gulping down a clump of green goodness, and flexing his pumped-up muscles to rescue Olive Oyl. New-school me? Women of God opening his Word, walking out their calling, and displaying incredible faith and courage through trials and tribulations. We are those women because Jesus rescued us.

I think we might struggle with the term "strong" because the world's perspective differs from the biblical perspective. When things get hard, we're often told to be strong which to me equates to stuffing down emotions instead of awakening to feel what we need to feel. When distractions come, when life gets busy, we seem to go through life asleep, missing what's real and right in front of us. How many times does fear hold us back from experiencing the abundant life we already have? We fear the future—will we have enough, be enough, do enough—but the key is not "will," it is "what."

Pray and think on these questions then write your answers below them.

What do you already have above material, temporal things?

In what ways has God already used you to help others?

What brings you joy right now?

Just like seven-year-old me and my bad dreams, fear can keep us bound in a sleep state. When we face fear down and force our eyes open, we discover the joy Jesus already gave us *his joy* that our joy might be full and that's a promise straight from John 15:11.

We can awaken to the great joy we've already been given. Let's walk this journey together—wide-awake and aware of how we fit into God's big-picture story.

Day Two: Renewing Our Soul Awakens Our Joy

Awakening to Our Need for Ongoing Soul Care

Scripture-fed prayer for the journey: Psalm 23

While walking along the streets of St. Petersburg, Florida, with my hubby, the strap of my favorite sandals broke. The sole flipped backward, separating from my foot, and almost sending me tumbling to the ground—not my finest moment. I had to think of a quick fix until I could buy another pair. This called for some creativity! What was the temporary fix? A hairband. I found a hairband at the bottom of my purse and bound the sole of the sandal to my foot. The temporary fix wasn't ideal but sufficed for a time.

When my sandal strap broke, the quick fix could not sustain my stride forever. It's like that with us and Jesus. When we experience busyness and brokenness in everyday life, our connection to Jesus can feel broken too. Reading a short devotional or singing a worship song might be a temporary fix for our souls but will not sustain us for the long-haul journey ahead. We must abide in Jesus, the true vine, to keep our souls refreshed and cared for. We need Jesus for true soul care because Jesus cares for our soul.

The True Essence of the Soul

According to the *Bible Sense Lexicon* reference, the soul (Hebrew word: *nephesh*/Greek word: *psychē*) means life or being, with an ultimate source in God. Our souls are the immaterial part of a person which is the actuating cause of an individual life—the site of all the psychological faculties (such as the heart, mind, and conscience).[1]

Here's more insight into the soul found in this quote by Joel T. Hamme:

The soul is the life-force of the person and often refers to the whole being. It needs to be sustained in order for life to thrive, and it is the seat of desires, emotions, and the will. The soul can be in intimate relationship with God or be under God's judgment.[2]

How does John 15 relate to our soul care? There is no right or wrong answer here. After reading this chapter, list below the ways this passage of Scripture relates to our soul care:

We might attempt to quench the thirst of our ailing souls with a nap, lunch with a friend, or a vacation. Naps are wonderful, but how often has a nap left us feeling more tired? Lunches with friends are delightful, but an hour of conversation can leave us wanting more. We all love vacations, but the travel part can be arduous. Amen? True soul care goes much deeper, and self-care is not the same as soul care. Soul care comes through abiding in the vine and abiding in his love. Soul care is when we honor God, put him first, and leave no open doors to sin.

Read Ephesians 4:27. What does this verse instruct us not to do?

Falling into sin is the quickest way to deplete the vitality of our souls. When we get too busy to abide in the vine every day, sin can easily beset us. A distant relationship from the vine will dry up our we-are-the-branches souls faster than we can say uh-oh. We know when we're in trouble—we can feel when our souls are moving farther and farther away from our life-source, our vine. We can see the cycle here and our need for daily soul care.

Each of us has a weakness—the sin we're tempted with and could succumb to if we're not abiding in the vine. Before sin comes temptation, and what tempts you might not tempt me, but one thing common to many of us is unforgiveness. Our flesh finds forgiveness hard to offer because offenses cut deep. We hold onto unforgiveness because we believe forgiving means they're off the hook, scot-free, let off easy. We believe forgiving them is saying what they did was okay, but forgiveness is not about that. Through Jesus, our sins are forgiven when we repent and ask for forgiveness. Only God has the power to forgive sin. Forgiveness doesn't mean what we did was okay, but repentance cleanses us of our sin. When people sin against us, it is God who can forgive their sin—that's between them and God—but through his grace alone we can forgive their offense against us. Unforgiveness is toxic to our souls. Whether they've asked for your forgiveness or not, and even if the offense is great, and even though you might not forget, you have the power to forgive through God's grace. They might still be in sin, but when we forgive, we release the ties that bind us to them. They aren't getting off scot-free—rather we are experiencing freedom from any hold they've had over us. Besides all of that, unforgiveness in God's economy is not an option. He has the authority and power to forgive sins, and he has taught us to forgive offenses against us because we have been forgiven. We see this in The Lord's Prayer, the model prayer Jesus taught us.

> Pray then like this: 'Our Father in heaven, hallowed be your name. Your kingdom come, your will be done, on earth as it is in heaven. Give us this day our daily bread, and forgive us our debts, as we also have forgiven our debtors. And lead us not into temptation, but deliver us from evil.' (Matthew 6:9–13)

In this prayer, Jesus says, "forgive us our debts, as we also have forgiven our debtors." A powerful truth Jesus teaches because he cares for our souls. Luke 11:4 records a shorter version of the prayer but with just as powerful a message on forgiveness. Luke 11:4 reads, "**and forgive us our sins, for we ourselves forgive everyone who is indebted to us. And lead us not into temptation.**"

We can make two important observations from the above passages of Scripture:

1. In Matthew, Jesus shows us we ask God to forgive us in present tense, but our forgiving others is in past tense. We've already forgiven others when we ourselves ask for forgiveness. We have forgiven and we will be forgiven.
2. In Luke, Jesus taught us to say, "we ourselves forgive everyone." We forgive everyone. Everyone.

In both passages "And lead us not into temptation" immediately follows the message on forgiveness. We are tempted to forgo forgiveness, among other things, so we must ask God to lead us from temptation, including the temptation to hold onto unforgiveness.

Surrender the Joy Stealers

We become healthy disciples who make disciples when we practice soul care, by ridding our souls of toxicity and abiding in Jesus every day. Write a prayer below, asking the Lord to minister to your soul and show you how to abide and allow Jesus to care for your soul.

Day Three: Renewing Our Spirit Awakens Our Joy

Awakening to Our Need for Knowing God Intimately

Scripture-fed prayer for the journey: Psalm 51:10

As a young mom, getting kids off to school and me to work felt like a three-ring circus. On one such crazy morning, I was not just running late but running on empty. I trusted God for the first several miles to work, praying I wouldn't run out of gas. But just half a mile from my destination, I caved. I pulled into the gas station, experiencing what I thought was a fear-over-faith-epic-fail. To top that, my bank account needed a refill too. I had a five-dollar balance soon to be gobbled up by a five-dollar outstanding check. I felt I didn't have a choice and pumped that bank overdraft straight into my gas tank.

Panic overtook me when I arrived at work with less than a minute to spare. As a banker, overdrawing your checking account was almost as bad as robbing the bank! Okay, maybe not to that extreme, but overdrafts were frowned upon and cause for possible disciplinary action. If that wasn't bad enough, I felt double-minded guilty. I prayed to get to work without running out of gas, then I ran out of faith just a sprint from the finish line.

By no coincidence, the president of the bank was a guest at our team meeting that morning. As we gathered in the lobby, I took a seat, feeling both ashamed and unworthy. He asked a question about our secret shopper program—where people pose as customers and rate employees on the service they received. I was the only one to raise a hand. After answering correctly, he was so pleased he pulled out his wallet. He said lunch was on him and he handed me a five-dollar bill.

Before you call him a cheapskate, back then five dollars bought a halfway decent lunch. However, lunch was not the true prize here. As I reached for that five-dollar bill, he probably wondered why I looked as though I'd never seen one before. What he didn't know was that five-dollar bill meant more to me than a twenty, a hundred, or even a thousand-dollar bill would have in that moment—because I knew without a doubt God saw me, he knew my exact need, and he met my need. *El Roi*, the God who sees me, saw me at the gas pump. He didn't think my concerns were trivial—and he didn't think my faith had failed.

Our trust and faith might waiver at times, but God is always trustworthy and faithful. It is God who provides, and he provided exactly what I needed at the exact moment I needed it. That is a God who knows us intimately and the beauty of this relationship is, we can know him intimately too. I love this quote by J. I. Packer from his book *Knowing God* ...

> What makes life worthwhile is having a big enough objective, something which catches our imagination and lays hold of our allegiance, and this the Christian has in a way that no other person has. For what higher, more exalted, and more compelling goal can there be than to know God.[3]

How is John 15 a picture of knowing God intimately?

What is your five-dollar bill story, when God made his undeniable presence known to you?

Have you encountered God intimately? If yes, share a time below. If not, write a prayer to God expressing your desire to know him intimately.

Be encouraged, friend! God sees you right where you are, and he creates in us clean hearts and renews steadfast spirits within us—and we can take that to the bank.

Day Four: Renewing Our Empowerment Awakens Our Joy

Awakening to the Indwelling of the Holy Spirit

Scripture-fed prayer for the journey: John 15: 5–15

In Francis Chan's book, *Forgotten God: Reversing Our Tragic Neglect of the Holy Spirit*, he says, "Empowering His children with the strength of the Holy Spirit is something the Father wants to do. It's not something we have to talk Him into. He genuinely wants to see us walk in His strength."[4]

Still wondering about whether you are bearing fruit? We bear much fruit when we abide in Christ, stick close to him, and are sensitive to the Spirit's leading. In Week Six we'll talk more about bearing much fruit, but for now, we can be confident in Christ that when we abide in him, fruit will bloom. Through Christ and the indwelling of the Holy Spirit, evidence of the fruit of the Spirit is displayed. This is how we love our neighbors well and glorify the Father. However, we are in a battle not only against the Enemy of our soul but against our own flesh-driven desires.

Read Galatians 5:16–23

How can we avoid walking in the desires of our flesh?

List the fruits of the Spirit below.

These fruits along with our gifting helps us live out our callings as we walk in the Spirit. When we are in Christ, we've been given gifts—spiritual gifts. There are Scripture verses naming these gifts, but for now, we'll talk about motivational gifts. We find them in Romans, chapter twelve, which we'll list later. These are the gifts that motivate us and get us excited about our role in kingdom work. As Christ-followers, we have at least one spiritual gift, but perhaps several. How are we using them? Are we using them? Our gifts are key to how God uses us to bear much fruit.

Abiding in the vine is vital—he is our lifeline to living and fruit-bearing. These gifts are supernatural God-tools he's equipped us with to use in kingdom work. There is a huge void within the Body of Christ when we leave our God-given spiritual gifts sitting on a table unwrapped.

What gifts have you been given for kingdom work? One thing to avoid regarding gifts is comparison. I have the gifts of encouragement and teaching, so I'm not your girl if you need your pantry organized or a meal team leader. I can organize, cook a meal, and lead, but they're not my strengths. I love having my Italian family dinners where the volume level of conversation could wake the dead. Lasagna is my specialty, and my family requests it on holidays. Just one pan can feed an army, and I enjoy seeing the people I love enjoy my lasagna. Still, I don't want to make the dish every day—can I get an amen? Yet, we all have at least one friend who loves whipping up meals and would bake, broil, fry, or grill 24/7 if she could. I used to want to love cooking, but I don't anymore, and that's okay. You might not want to either, and that's okay too. But be assured, even if you don't have the gift of hospitality, you have at least one spiritual gift.

Surrender the Joy Stealers | 125

Read 1 Corinthians 12:11. Who distributes the gifts?

Do you know what your gifts are? There is more than one spiritual gift list in the Bible, but we'll focus on the motivational gift list in Romans.

Read Romans 12:6–8 and write the gifts named in this list below.

Your gifts are meant to be used where your passion, compassion, and conviction intersect, which is what I call your fierce calling. Can you identify with these gifts and which ones you have? You know when you're operating in your gifting. Your gifts are what people have observed about you as well. We can't all have the same gift or things would never get done. However, many can have the same gift, and because they are fearfully, wonderfully, and uniquely made by the hand of God, no two people will use the same gift in the same way.

In a sermon a few years ago, one of our pastors presented a spiritual gifts illustration. He was teaching on the gifts in Romans and how they might be used. Inspired by the sermon, I created my own illustration. I hope you enjoy seeing how each of these women have been called to use the gifts they've been given.

SPIRITUAL GIFTS ILLUSTRATION:

Samantha serves on the Women's Ministry team. On a sunny Saturday morning, a roomful of women sits listening to the conference speaker while enjoying grilled chicken salads topped with candied pecans with a dash of raspberry vinaigrette. Desserts were up next on the event schedule, and Samantha, having the gift of serving, slips out of the kitchen with a trayful of delicious treats. While heading toward the dessert table, her heal catches a snag in the carpeting and Samantha and her tray of delectable delights go flying. A mini eclair lands in Jennifer's coffee, cookies crumble across the floor, and chunks of brownie find a home in Julie's hair. Several women, all with different spiritual gifts, rush to the rescue.

Olivia, with the gift of prophesy, suggests Samantha make two trips next time or perhaps consider asking others for help carrying the desserts. At first, we might think she's rude, but we need her gift. The gift of prophesy brings correction, shares messages of truth, and challenges false teaching our culture might be drawing us to believe. Olivia insists on obedience to God and his word. Olivia is a truth-teller and tells the truth in love.

Christine has the gift of serving. She's picking the brownie chunks from Julie's hair and after the event, she'll be the one vacuuming up the cookie crumbs.

Felicia has the gift of teaching. She's the one on the platform teaching the message God laid on her heart. She also teaches a class at church on Wednesday nights.

Mandy has the gift of exhortation—also referred to as encouragement. She extends a hand to Samantha, helping her up while telling her she's doing a great job and encouraging her to get right back in the game. She assures Samantha there are still enough desserts and thanks her for serving.

Dana has the gift of giving. She gives with a grateful heart and donates to the Women's Ministry to replace the loss. She loves and feels called to financially support kingdom work.

Valerie has the gift of leadership. She's taking charge and delegating tasks like seeing what additional snacks the team can round up to serve the ladies. She also gets the event back on track by directing the focus back onto the speaker. Valerie is the gal making sure the event ends on time.

Celeste has the gift of mercy. She is drawn to anyone needing assistance—she's following behind Samantha to make sure she's okay.

Which one of these roles resonates with you and why?

Group exercise idea:

Allow time for each woman in your group to share which role she saw herself in. You might even present your own skit or create a similar illustration. Have fun with it!

DAY FIVE: RENEWING OUR MINDS AWAKENS OUR JOY

AWAKENING TO OUR TRANSFORMATION THROUGH THE WORD OF GOD

Scripture-fed prayer for the journey: Romans 12:2

In *Switch On Your Brain: The Key to Peak Happiness, Thinking and Health,*[5] Dr. Caroline Leaf shares how she was inspired by Romans 12:2 to teach her patients how to renew their minds. All actions begin with a thought and the Bible gives us instructions on navigating our thought-life and what we are to think on.

What does Romans 12:2 tell us not to do?

How are we to be transformed?

Romans 8:27—How does the Spirit help us?

Read the following Scriptures. What do these verses instruct us about right thinking?
2 Corinthians 10:1–6 & Philippians 4:8

Isaiah 26:3

Luke 10:27

Romans 8:5–7

2 Corinthians 13:11

Ephesians 4:17–24

Philippians 4:6–7

How can we have perfect peace? By keeping our minds on Jesus. How can our minds be renewed day by day? Through reading the truth of God's word.

BACK TO THE VINE

Here are practical practices for taking thoughts captive and replacing them with truth:

- Write Bible verses on index cards and carry them with you
- Write Bible verses on sticky notes and stick them on your mirrors
- Sing your favorite worship songs aloud or in your mind. We can't think unholy thoughts while singing praises to God, right? Creating a playlist is a wonderful action you can take!

- Text a trusted friend or spiritual mentor for prayer. Accountability helps us to be intentional in our thinking and helps us replace unhealthy thoughts with God's truth.

What has God revealed to you during this week's study?

LISTEN

Fierce Calling Podcast episode #114
Anjuli Paschall: "Awakening to the Full Life God has Already Given You"
https://dorisswift.com/2022/08/16/anjuli-paschall-awakening-to-the-full-life-god-has-already-given-you/

Fierce Calling Podcast episode #17
Tara Cole: "The Busy Mom's Guide to Connecting with God"
https://dorisswift.com/2020/02/25/17-the-busy-moms-guide-to-connecting-with-god-with-guest-tara-cole/

WEEK FIVE: REST

Introduction: Rest in This Truth: When We Seek Rest, We Will Find It

Scripture-fed prayer for the journey: Matthew 11:29

When was the last time you felt rested? Not just powernap rested, but *down-to-your-soul* rested? I think I can speak for both of us when I say we're a weary bunch of travelers on this road called life on earth. Our souls thirst for rest, but what does resting well even mean? Have we ever learned how? Our schedules are full, and although what's on them are good things, there's a difference between full and fulfilled. We're missing the mark if our version of rest is happy hour at Dunkin's or eating out so we don't have to cook, both of which I love. Why is there so much guilt tied to rest? As if we can't sit for one minute without the dishes in the sink and clothes in the dryer mocking us until we tend to them. Some might see resting as laziness but let's be real, we get lazy because we've fallen out of rest. God taught us what rest looks like—we create beauty, and then, we step back and take a rest. Our need for rest is much deeper than getting enough sleep or taking a vacation a few weeks out of the year. Our need for rest extends from our need to rest in him.

Day One: Rest for Our Bodies

Finding Sabbath Rest

Scripture-fed prayer for the journey: Matthew 11:28–30

When we purchased a new refrigerator, I was surprised to discover the appliance included a Sabbath mode. Even my refrigerator observes the Sabbath! According to the instructions, this mode can disable sounds, timers, and interior lighting which made an impact on me. This action reminds me to remember the Sabbath and keep it holy, especially when I reach for the unsweetened iced tea. The struggle to rest is real, amen?

Traditionally, Sundays are considered the day of rest for many Christians. I used to consider attending church an obligation, another task to check off my good-girl to-do list. My distorted perspective of church attendance made Sundays feel anything but restful. I used to ask myself: why attend church? Why can't we just stay home and rest? Isn't God everywhere anyway? These are all valid questions, and perhaps you've asked them too. What is the best way to find answers? Ask. As I matured in my walk with Christ, I sought answers from God. Yes, God is everywhere, and we can meet with him anywhere—but everything God calls us to has purpose. God opened my eyes to see church not as an obligation or a to-do list task—but as a gathering with purpose.

A change in perspective can happen when we read this verse:

> And let us consider how to stir up one another to love and good works, not neglecting to meet together, as is the habit of some, but encouraging one another, and all the more as you see the Day drawing near. (Hebrews 10:24–25)

What do you glean from this verse?

Look up the word "obligation" in your paperback or online dictionary. What is the main gist in the definitions you've found?

Church is not meant to feel like an obligation, but rather an invitation to living on mission. Isn't it more fulfilling to experience church as restoration? Church is not just about checking a box because we have to be there but being there to stir up one another to love and good works.

That sounds restful to me, how about you?

When we accept Christ, we become children of God—part of a family gathering to encourage one another in love and support. We're equipped by the Word and worship in unison preparing us for what we'll face Monday through Saturday—life in the world. Attending church isn't about a building, but about a people. The building isn't the church, we're the church. Isn't gathering with like-minded people like drawing in a breath of fresh air? Lord knows there's plenty of opposition out there, and that gets exhausting, right?

When we get to our family reunion of believers on Sundays, or whatever days you gather, we are reminded of our hope for the future. We learn together how to reach the lost for Christ. We learn we were never meant to go it alone because we were made for community with the Father, Son, and Holy Spirit, and with our brothers and sisters in Christ. As we share the gospel, our family grows, and we live out our purpose together. We experience refreshment and rest for our souls when walking in our calling and living out a purposeful and fruitful life.

Maybe your experience in church has not been a good one. Church hurts, spiritual abuse, and unhealthy leadership can leave you disillusioned about the concept of church. If this is you, I understand where you're coming from, and more importantly, so does God. You are the church gathered if you're going through this study with a group of Jesus followers. Yet God might have new opportunities for you on the horizon. Seek his will, and if that has you journeying back to a church body, he'll lead you to a church that's the right fit for you. No church is perfect because it's full of imperfect people. But those with a heart for loving like Jesus and being missional at heart can make all the difference.

To make things clear, going to church doesn't save us, but gathering with other believers does refresh our souls and encourages our spirits. Church is a training ground—a boot-camp if you will—for the Lord's army. We learn to armor-up and get down to business, God's business. The verse we read in Hebrews is inviting us to consider our part in the body of Christ. The writer invites us to consider how important each believer's role is in kingdom work. The verse also calls some people out, amen? They know who they are, so let's not be them. Romans 12:4–5 solidifies our kingdom workers membership.

> For as in one body we have many members, and the members do not all have the same function, so we, though many, are one body in Christ, and individually members one of another.

HONORING GOD THROUGH SABBATH REST

Sabbath rest doesn't mean sleeping all day or lazing around on the couch, although such behavior is not unacceptable. Sabbath rest goes much deeper. Perhaps you love gardening, and you feel close to God while digging your hands into the rich soil. Gardening might be your expression of Sabbath rest. Me, not so much. I have the brownest thumbs on the planet, and while I love to see and smell God's beautiful creations, I'm not called to plant flowers. I am, however, called to plant seeds in people, and at times water seeds others have planted. You are too. I'm glad I don't need green thumbs for that, just the Holy Spirit's leading and guidance. We do the planting, watering, and caring and he brings the transformation. We all make a great team, don't we?

Read 1 Corinthians 3:6–8.

Who gives the growth?

What do waterers and planters have in common?

We might plant the seeds, or we might water them—either way, isn't it exciting how these actions can be the answer to someone else's prayer. Are you praying for a loved one to be saved? Me too. I am thankful for planters and waterers God sends to them. Jesus was out doing kingdom work on the Sabbath, healing a man with a withered hand in Matthew 12:10, disregarding the accusatory fingers of the pharisees, and telling them and us (see Matthew 12:12) doing good on the Sabbath is lawful and right. Jesus shows us how people are always to be valued over legalistic practices, including on the Sabbath.

Keeping the Sabbath Holy

In Hebrew, the word Sabbath means "day of rest" and is commandment number four of the ten commandments. We are to keep the Sabbath holy, and as followers of Jesus, we find the true meaning of Sabbath rest in him. Jesus became our ultimate Sabbath rest because he sacrificed himself for us. We find no rest in our sins, but through the blood of Christ, we were washed clean.

Sabbath rest is not just about avoiding work on a Sunday, but about remembering the one who did the work for us so we could be free. Finding rest for our bodies on the Sabbath is just a part of what true rest means. We can rest while walking with him, talking with him, and knowing that only through Jesus can we find our Sabbath rest because he lives.

Read Matthew 12:8 and record below the name given to Jesus in this verse:

Read Hebrews 4:9–11 and write your thoughts on this passage below:

Rest in Jesus and ask him what he would have you to do in observance of the Sabbath. In the Old Testament, each way the Sabbath was observed pointed to preparing for a coming Messiah. In Exodus 16:22–30 God gave instruction in preparing his people for the Sabbath. Jesus changes everything for us—we are still called to remember the Sabbath and keep it holy—but Jesus is our Sabbath rest. When we are in him, he is all we need.

Day Two: Rest for Our Souls

Finding Rest in God Alone

Scripture-fed prayer for the journey: Exodus 33:14

God's presence gives us rest. We find rest for our souls when we live and serve from a place of rest. Jesus invites us to come to him and find rest. Rest for our souls is about cultivating an intimacy with God who wants a relationship with us. Unrest for our souls is neglecting our relationship with God which leads to the inability to resist the temptations of this world. The Enemy wants unrest for your soul. He wants to trip you up, then take you out. He dangles carrots in front of our faces, the ones we can't resist without God's help. God hasn't moved—we're the ones who move. The further from our intimacy with God, the further the journey is back to him—and the Enemy is waiting for a foothold.

Read Ephesians 4:25–5:2 and summarize what the Holy Spirit reveals to you in this passage:

The Enemy wants a foothold in our lives. Once we give him an in, getting him out is hard. James 4:7 tells us when we submit to God and resist the devil, he'll flee from us. Easier said than done! We tend to forget the submit to God part and want to run right to the we resist you, devil, part. When we do that, he doesn't go anywhere. Submitting to God is key for our soul care. What does that look like? Yielding to God in total submission. Allowing our hearts to look to God as first in our lives, because heaven knows, sometimes we've put him in last place. We don't mean to, but we get busy, tired, discouraged, and we forget whose we are. Our soul care, our soul rest, and our soul health come from the ultimate source of our soul, resting in Jesus.

The Enemy won't have an open door to wedge his foot into when we submit our lives to God, talk with him, read his Word, and draw near in the intimacy of fellowshipping with him. When we don't, he and his rats-to-garbage demons will harass us and make our lives miserable. There's nothing restful about that, but we don't have to surrender to Satan's efforts when we've surrendered all to God. Sin brings shame, guilt, and a soul crying for help. Thankfully, the Holy Spirit is our helper, and he does not condemn us but convicts us of sin so we can call out to God for forgiveness and slam those sin doors shut.

When is the last time you felt rested way down to your soul? Let's end our time together today by writing a prayer of submission to God. In our personal prayers, let's confess and ask forgiveness for any open doors to the Enemy, and ask for God's help to forgive those we might be harboring unforgiveness against. Once we've worked through those things, we can ask God to bring refreshment to our souls.

Day Three: Rest Assured

Finding Our Security in the God Who Provides

Scripture-fed prayer for the journey: Philippians 4:19

Remember in Week Two when I shared about the time Brian injured his back? I touched on the main points, but there's more to the story which brings God glory. You might recall he was out of work for an entire month—a major financial setback for us. What I had not yet shared was since we already depleted our savings, all I could think of to do was to sell my three-stone diamond ring. I loved that ring—a meaningful birthday gift from Brian. Ring in hand, I practically dragged myself into the jewelry store to see how little a value they would place on something priceless to me.

I didn't sell my ring to them—I just couldn't bring myself to do it. I walked right back out of the store, but I knew if I needed to sell my ring, God would make a way. I remember telling God how sorry I was about making the ring an idol. I used to get distracted in church, gazing down at three exquisite diamonds glistening in the sanctuary lights. However, a ring is not eternal—only a temporal band of polished stones wedged in metal. The true value came from the giver—my hubs who was down for the count. This was not about me or the ring, but about getting us through a difficult season, and this is the thought I had—what if God provided the ring then, knowing I would need it now?

Once I changed my perspective and released the three-diamond idol from my finger, God provided a family member to buy my ring, not because she wanted the ring but because she wanted to help. I can't tell you how relieved I was about keeping that ring in the family.

God is all about restoration, and if he chooses to give me another ring down the road, I will receive it with joy.

I'm not looking for a ring, though, because the sweetest gifts are unexpected blessings. Not long after I let my ring go, and when I least expected it, a heartfelt card with a check tucked inside arrived in the mailbox from a sister in Christ. God is our Jehovah Jirah—our provider. He knows what we need, and he provides for that need at just the right time. We can trust him because he always keeps his promises. He also knows what we don't need, even when we think we do, and we can trust him with those things too.

THE WIDOW'S OIL

I love the story of the prophet Elisha and the widow in need found in 2 Kings 4:1–7. Head on over there and read the passage. Share your thoughts below:

The world will tell us our security is found in money, other people, and whatever else makes us feel secure about the future. Our true security is found in Christ alone. He has secured our future with him and in him. God provides all our needs.

Day Four: Restoration in Our Relationship with the Father

Finding Joy in Our Salvation

Scripture-fed prayer for the journey: Psalm 51
Make Psalm 51 your prayer.

She awoke that day without an inkling of what awaited her. She began her journey seeking water from a well and ended up finding a wellspring of living water. She became the waterpot as joy overflowed from her and she could not contain it.

Let's read her story in John 4:1–42

Note in verses 3 and 4 that Jesus was heading to Galilee, and verse 4 says, "And he had to pass through Samaria." Jews avoided going through Samaria, opting to go around instead of through a place they despised. There was a history of bad blood between the Jews and Samaritans, who had their own belief system, mixing Judaism with idolatry.

Why then does verse 4 say Jesus had to pass through Samaria?

We've all been the woman at the well. Our stories might be different, but our need for a Savior is the same. Friend, Jesus journeyed into our Samaria to rescue us too. What is your woman at the well story? Where was your well when he found you there?

Write your story below.

Day Five: Rested and Ready

Finding How Rest Readies us for Divine Appointments

Scripture-fed prayer for the journey: 2 Timothy 4:2

She walked into the church office thirty minutes before closing time. Young, desperate, and looking for hope, she pleaded for a ride to the airport. She'd been kicked to the curb by her so-called boyfriend, and all the belongings she owned on earth were crammed into a carry-on. You hear everything over the years when you work in a church office. The common-thread stories that are just that—stories. Yet there was something different and endearing about this girl. She asked if there was somewhere she could freshen up, so I pointed her to the restroom down the hall. She grabbed her bag and headed that way as I hit the phone. I was the only one in the office, so I couldn't drive her to the airport. After several calls, I found someone who could—a friend in the city south of us who had a ministry to battered women. She answered, I explained the situation, and she didn't hesitate for a second—she'd be there in fifteen minutes.

Relieved, I hung up the phone just as my visitor returned to the office. I shared the good news, and she was grateful. Any doubts I might have had about her story of being a pastor's daughter and raised in the church soon vanished. She plopped down in a chair and unzipped her suitcase, digging for something buried at the bottom. I watched as she flung clothing and other contents onto the floor, digging for God knows what. Then, her eyes widened and smiling big, she held it up high. Her pink, Precious Moments Bible her mother had given her as a child. She kept that treasured Bible with her through all her trauma and all her wandering. I had no doubt this sweet prodigal would return to who she knows—Jesus. I prayed with her, and I knew, as she walked out that door, this divine appointment was an answer to prayer for people who love her.

I asked her to please update me on how she was doing—but I haven't heard from her. Thankfully, God knows where she is right at this very moment, and I trust he has his hand upon her life. I know why God led her into the church office that day. She needed the hands and feet of Jesus to pray with her, listen to her, have compassion for her, and get her to that airport.

Divine appointments happen all the time, but if we're too weary for well-doing, we'll miss them.

Read Galatians 6:9. What does Paul advise us?

BACK TO THE VINE

Write John 15:12 below.

Weary one, don't give up. God has work for us to do! Although life can be hard, we must rest and allow God to refresh and ready us for divine appointments. We are called to love others and showing love can come in many different forms. Yes, it had been a long day by the time my Precious Moments Bible visitor rang the church office doorbell. Good thing I was prayed up and willing for God to use me to meet her need. As tired as I might have been, that divine appointment energized my soul, blessing me as much as she was blessed—by God. And there are so many more stories of so many more divine appointments—all we need to do is be willing. All we need to do is say yes to God and he will fill our divine appointment calendars with precious moments we can treasure forever.

What divine appointments has God sent your way?

Write a prayer asking God to refresh your soul and ready you for the work he prepared in advance for you to do (see Ephesians 2:10).

LISTEN

Fierce Calling Podcast episode #33
Amber Cullum: "The Good Fruit of Comparison and Sabbath Rest"
https://dorisswift.com/2020/06/16/33-the-good-fruit-of-comparison-and-sabbath-rest/

Fierce Calling Podcast episode #67
Sarah Keeling: "Simple Psalm Prayers and Finding True Rest in God"
https://dorisswift.com/2021/09/14/sarah-keeling-simple-psalm-prayers-and-finding-true-rest-in-god/

WEEK SIX: REACH

What is All This Fruit Meant For?

Introduction: Living Missionally Through Bearing and Sharing Much Fruit

Scripture-fed prayer: John 15:26–27

I used to think being a missionary meant traveling to foreign lands and learning new languages to share the gospel to the ends of the earth. While that is true, being a missionary means so much more. As followers of Christ, we are all on mission wherever we are because the truth is, we are all living in a foreign land. Even if we never step foot on what we consider foreign soil, we are all foreigners here on earth. In her book *Far from Home: Discovering Your Identity as Foreigners on Earth*,[1] my friend Mabel Ninan shares how feeling like foreigners in the world we live in is natural—we're just passing through—and while we're here, we have work to do.

Remember when we talked about how our spiritual gifts are distributed to us by the Holy Spirit? He also helps us in pairing our gifts with our calling so we can bear much fruit. This reminds me of the word "cultivate" which often refers to preparing the soil for planting a future harvest. God cultivates in us everything we need to walk in whatever ministry he calls us to. He helps us break up our fallow ground, the hard dry places within us, so good things can grow in our hearts. He prepares us for working in the mission fields of life, and if we do not quit, we will reap a harvest as we read last week in Galatians 6:9.

Do you consider yourself a missionary? Why or why not?

In Acts 13:47, Jesus doesn't suggest, but commands us to go forth as lights in the world to share the gospel to the ends of the earth. The entire planet earth is a mission field, and wherever you live, your home is included in the ends of the earth. You are a missionary meant to light up the world for Christ whether you're called to a mission field across the ocean or across the street. What if we all lived like the lights that we are? Think of the impact we could make together—far reaching and fruitful.

Day One: Living Missionally in Our Homes

Bearing Fruit that Stays Fresh for Generations

Scripture-fed prayer for the journey: John 15:16–17

On my way to a friend's house, I drove past what used to be a popular fruit stand. Once a well-known landmark in our community, the building now sits run-down and abandoned. I'm not sure if I ever stopped there while the fruit stand was open, or if they've moved elsewhere, but I loved seeing the vibrant colors of fresh fruit piled high in baskets out front. Abundant offerings from an abundant harvest. Now all that remains is an empty shell of a weather-worn building no longer bearing vibrant fruit. Not a breath of life is anywhere to be found. This building is a reminder of what can happen to us if we hold back the gifts we've been given—we miss bearing vibrant fruit and we miss breathing life-giving words into future generations.

What was sown into us as we became the future generation? Whether raised in a broken, fruitless home, or a fruitful one, our true source of fruit-bearing abundance flows from our home in heaven. Isn't that encouraging? We are all on an even playing field when it comes to bearing much fruit, because we're all children of God. Fresh starts, fresh purpose, and fresh fruit is produced in and through us by God himself. As missionaries, we are equipped and empowered to engage our gifts in bearing fruit in our homes—fruit that stays fresh for generations.

Turn to Proverbs 22:6 and write the verse below.

What is our role according to this verse?

If we do this, what happens?

Even children raised in a Christian home might stray from the way they should go. Many of us did for a time too, amen? Maybe you're praying for a prodigal—that child you trained up who walked away from the faith. That alone is enough to crumble a mama's heart and steal your joy, but your mama's heart is stronger than you think. And joy is here to stay because Jesus placed his joy in you that your joy may be full. Our joy is always full, prodigals and all.

When we raise our children in the faith, there comes a time when faith must become their own. Children can't ride on the coattails of a parent's faith because their faith won't be genuine, and imitation faith won't stick.

Read Isaiah 55:11

What is the promise in this verse?

We aren't perfect—far from it—but we know God's word is true. Our role is to follow Jesus and teach what we know and live what we teach.

Read Deuteronomy 6:4–9

What should we teach our children and when?

What about children not raised Christian homes? That's where the church comes in. As Christians, we're called to sow into the next generation. There are countless testimonies of children trained up in the way they should go by Sunday School teachers, church camp leaders, and neighbors who share Jesus over milk and cookies. God's design is for parents to instill God's truth into the lives of their kids, but not all parents know Jesus. Still, many parents are good with their kids knowing Jesus. Sowing into the next generation bears much fruit, and some of the sweetest fruit is found when parents meet Jesus through their saved children. Is God calling you to serve in youth or children's ministries at your church?

The generations to come have been entrusted to us. God's grace is sufficient even if we missed the mark in Deuteronomy. While we can't make someone believe, and we can't make someone choose to follow Jesus, we can trust they can't unknow what they know, and they can't unlearn what they've learned. God's word of truth. God's word is in them no matter how old they get or how hard they try to forget. Things along the way in life's journey reminds them of what they've been taught. I believe the verse referenced in today's study, Isaiah 55:11, affirms for us God's word accomplishes his purpose in their lives. Isn't the story the sweetest when Jesus leaves the ninety-nine and goes after the one? That one lost sheep who has gone astray?

Read Matthew 18:10–14. What is most encouraging to you about this passage of Scripture?

God loves our loved ones far beyond our capacity to love them. He has plans for them and we can trust he wants what's best for them, even more than we do. Our prayers do not go unheard and since God tells us numerous times not to worry about *anything,* we must surrender every worry and the outcome to him. Surrendering our loved ones to God is the way we should go, and no matter how old we are, we should not depart from it.

Day Two: Living Missionally in Our Church

BEARING FRUIT IN MINISTRY

Scripture-fed prayer for the journey: John 15

How did you feel the first time you visited your current church? Did you feel welcomed? In 2001, God made clear I needed to find a church closer to home—one with an active youth group for our daughter. The church we attended was a thirty-minute drive, and their youth group dwindled after the youth pastor left. I explained to our then pastor and his wife we needed to find an active youth group, so we left with their blessings. Being the introvert that I am, I wasn't interested in "church hopping" so I prayed God would send us to the right church right off the bat. Edgewater Alliance Church was just seven minutes from our front door. On Palm Sunday 2001, I turned into that driveway and never looked back.

Karen was one of the first to greet me on that Sunday. When I returned the following Sunday, she greeted me again, by name, and I wasn't even wearing a name tag. After attending for several weeks, I became a member, and I joined that greeting team. I wanted to make people feel as welcomed, seen, and known as Karen made me feel.

My friend Karen has a gift for making people feel welcomed—like she's known you for years. I soon realized she did not keep this gift to herself. She'd pull me aside at church, point out a visitor, and say something like, "You see that woman in the red shirt? Would you please introduce yourself and get her name for me before she leaves today?" After a while, you realize Karen asked many of us to do the same thing. I know because we've compared notes. At first, we thought we were on a "Karen mission," meeting visitors to report back names. Then we realized the mission wasn't about reporting back names—

the mission was about connecting with people. We then helped them get connected—plugged in. Clusters of communities form and intentional communities become missional communities when you help people connect with other people.

The early church met in homes, and many believers still do. We are the church, not the buildings or the programs. Buildings and programs are resources for God's assets—us included. You might not think of yourself as an asset, but you are. All fruit-bearers are assets to the kingdom and useful in kingdom work.

Read Matthew 9:37 and 1 Corinthians 3:9

What is our role as stated in these verses?

We are assets to the harvest not because we're all that, but because we're all his. Yet are we all in? Being missional in our churches isn't intimidating—it's invigorating. Serve where your gifts have potential to make the most impact. Find the ministry work you were designed for—a true match made in heaven, after all. You might think being missional at church is like preaching to the choir.

Here are a few thoughts to consider.

- Not everyone who walks into church is walking with Jesus
- Not everyone at church is connecting in community outside of church
- Not everyone has caught the vision of harvest work

Gathering at church opens doors for divine connections. You meet women with a calling much like yours—to reach women in prison or children in schools. You strike up a conversation after Bible study, and lunch on Tuesdays become a regular thing. You get to know your server, and she gets to know Jesus. Church isn't an obligation, but an opportunity to find community, to grow in community. We can invite people into our churches but can also meet people where they are, and we can do it all together.

DAY THREE: LIVING MISSIONALLY IN OUR COMMUNITIES

BEARING FRUIT THROUGH MISSIONAL LIVING

Scripture-fed prayer for the journey: John 15:12

Annie makes a mean meatloaf—it's her thing. The dish isn't always meatloaf. The meal might be baked chicken or a hearty lasagna. Annie's ministry, Feed My Sheep, feeds hundreds of families. The beauty of this ministry is she isn't alone in making hearty meals with love, she invites other mad meatloaf makers to serve alongside her. That is missional living—loving and serving others well in community. God can use a warm meal to bring encouragement to their hearts and nourishment for their souls during some of the hardest seasons imaginable. That's Christ's love in action. A meal comforts the body, and compassion comforts the soul. When a believer offers someone a meal, this act of kindness tells them they are cared for, they are seen, and they are loved.

I know first-hand how a compassionate meal-maker brings joy and hope. Our entire home flooded when Hurricane Ian blasted Florida. Annie delivered a hot meal to warm our hearts. She drove up to my son's home, where we had fled to, armed with lasagna, garlic bread, and for dessert—ice cream and tiramisu. Her mission stems from her passion, compassion, and conviction to see people fed and feel loved. Mission accomplished. She gives all the glory to Jesus.

We face a long road of home repairs and rebuilding, and although what's been declared a disaster threatens to steal my joy, my circumstances cannot take ownership of my joy—which isn't transferable or up for grabs. My joy is constant, and Jesus placed his joy in me that my joy would be full—and full it is. How could anything else compare to Jesus's joy in us?

As hard as this season is, we're not alone in experiencing hardship. Our entire community piled personal belongings at the curb. Although the raging waters could not be contained, just a few days later, they were gone, but the devastation remained. Even so, God is still good, and I know he will restore what the locusts have eaten (see Joel 2:25) and will work this together for good for we who love him and are called according to his purpose (Romans 8:28).

What good can come by way of disaster? The answer: a community of neighbors who encourage one another. I long to know the women in my neighborhood on a deeper level, and once my home is livable again, my hope is to gather us together to share our stories. We all have a story, and our stories are not just about the storm. God can use a storm to open doors to healing, so he can make all things new again.

The storm brought a commonality of experiences, and although peeling wet photos apart and stuffing flood-drenched blouses into a trash bag is messy, God is in it all. He didn't cause the destruction, but he allowed these events to happen for reasons beyond what our eyes can see and our minds can know. He chooses to reveal his purposes in his timing, and it may not be this side of heaven—but we can see and know for sure God is good. God brings restoration after and even amid devastation because he is always at work in our lives. Through Christ in us we can shine brightly for him even when the lights go out.

We are lights, called to light up the dark with hope in Christ. A few years ago, I interviewed Sarah Harmeyer, founder of Neighbor's Table, on my podcast. Her love mission began in her own backyard when God placed a dream in her heart to gather people. She calls herself a "people gatherer." She invited her entire neighborhood to join her for a simple meal at a hand-crafted table made by her dad with love. If you invite them, they will come, right? Maybe not all of them, but those who show up are the ones meant to be there. Hundreds have enjoyed a hearty meal around Sarah's table.

We all crave community. Missional living is gathering others not just in community, but in unity. We might not all vote the same way or believe the same things, but when others experience genuine, unconditional love, it gets their attention. When they connect with us, they're connecting with Jesus because we're his hands and feet. When we gather with no agenda but to love well and share the hope we have, wonderful things can happen.

While meals bring us together, maybe cooking is not your thing. Maybe your gift is teaching. You could lead a Bible study with women in your neighborhood. Any woman can start a Bible study group. Here's the good news—we don't have to know everything before we step out and step up. We just need to know Jesus. So, here's your permission to step out, step up, and gather women who need community with other women. I think you already know a few.

Love to garden? How about a garden club? Love to read? How about a book club? Love to build and organize? Volunteer helping others with home repairs, organizing, and simplifying processes so people can thrive in day-to-day life. Being missional is about using whatever gifts, talents, and abilities God has blessed us with to bless others. Love in action opens doors to share God's love and hope in Christ—the gospel of peace.

What are your talents? What activities bring you joy?

How has God gifted you? List the ways you've been gifted below.

Looking back on your life, even as a child, how have you already been using these gifts and talents to bless others and point them to Jesus?

Our missional living doesn't have to look the same as Annie's way or Sarah's way. Maybe our missional living looks like meeting with a new neighbor over coffee or volunteering to coach a soccer team or helping an overwhelmed teacher in the classroom. Missional living is allowing God to expand our boarders in loving and serving all our neighbors, not just the ones who know him. When we do, sooner or later as we build relationships, opportunities to share about our most treasured relationship with Jesus will come. Through the building of relationships, our words hold greater impact because others will see the impact Jesus has made on our lives.

Read 1 Peter 3:15 and write below what strikes you about this verse.

Be ready and get ready because when we are willing, God multiplies divine appointments in our lives. Is there someone God has laid on your heart to call, text, or invite to lunch? When we get busy doing life, we're tempted to ignore those Holy Spirit nudges to connect, but those nudges come at the exact time someone needs it. Have we considered the ways God can use us as an answer to someone else's prayers? Let's not miss the opportunity. When we are in community with God, he shows us the community who needs to hear from him and about him. Have you felt a pull to lead a group in your home? At church? God has equipped you in past seasons so you can use what he's taught you in your current season. Our seasons of life change but missional living is always our calling.

As 1 John 4:19 says, we love because he first loved us, and we can love like Jesus because his love flows through us. This is a supernatural love because, although we are called to love everyone, sometimes that love doesn't come easy, amen? Yet we can love the unlovable because we've been soaked in God's grace. And those who don't yet know Jesus do not have the capacity to love like Jesus. They have not yet experienced the kind of love we all yearn for, and that's why sharing his love is a high calling. Lives are impacted for the kingdom when his love flows through us. Let's clothe ourselves in holy overalls and work side-by-side in the harvest.

Day Four: Living Missionally in Our Walk with Christ

Bearing Fruit as We Follow the Command to Make Disciples

Scripture-fed prayer for the journey: John 15:26–27

In just three years' time, Jesus called, equipped, and sent out his disciples to share the good news. How amazing it must have been to sit under his teachings! While Jesus is no longer with us in flesh, the gospel continues to spread because he trained leaders to train leaders.

What is Jesus's disciple-making model? We've covered discipleship in a previous week, but here's a quick review:

- Go to the ones God sends you to
- Spend time with them
- Pour into their lives by praying and studying the Bible together
- Allow them to observe how you live and how you walk with Jesus
- Observe their growth in how they walk with Jesus
- Release them to go to the ones God sends them to

That's it! We don't have to know everything to disciple someone. We just need to be a few steps ahead of someone to be qualified to teach. That goes for us too. We can always learn from someone a few steps ahead of us.

Read Titus 2:1–8 and circle how many times the word or root word teach is mentioned.

We might not all have the spiritual gift of teaching, but we can all teach what we've learned. What have you learned that made an impact on you? If you can't think of anything offhand, ask the Holy Spirit to bring something you've learned back to your remembrance. Write what comes to mind in the blank below.

Pray and ask the Lord about who he might be calling you to disciple. We need not worry about what we're to say or do because God equips us when we partner with him in kingdom work. Prayer is key in connecting with the heart of God. He shows us the way. In the space below, write down anything you feel the Lord is leading you to do or know. Write whatever he places on your heart.

Day Five: Living Missionally with the Fullness of Joy

Bearing Fruit, Sharing Fruit, and Cultivating the Fruit of the Spirit

Scripture-fed prayer for the journey: John 15

On this last day of the last week of our study, let's get back to the vine and delve into John 15 to review what we've studied. Then we'll create a Missional Living Plan.

Read John 15

Who is ...

the true vine?

the vinedresser?

the branch?

What does the vinedresser do?

Why does the vinedresser do this?

How many times does Jesus use the word or a form of the word "abide"?

Who and/or what does Jesus tell us to abide in?

When we abide, what happens?

When we do not abide, what happens?

What does Jesus command us to do?

What does Jesus call us besides branches in this passage?

Who chose whom?

What were we chosen to do?

What does Jesus teach us about the world?

Why does this matter?

Who is the Helper?

What does Jesus tell us about the Helper?

What does Jesus tell us in John 15:11?

As you look over your answers above, create a Missional Living Plan below. This is your personal plan, including who Jesus says you are and in what ways you can live out John 15. I'll provide a guide below, but please feel free to create your own version on a blank sheet of paper.

WHO JESUS SAYS I AM:

WHAT JESUS COMMANDS ME TO DO:

WAYS I WILL USE MY GIFTS IN MISSIONAL LIVING:

SIGNATURE: _____

Living on mission with Jesus doesn't mean your circumstances will always be ideal. Life is hard, but when we learn to surrender our joy stealers and walk in fullness of joy, we can redirect our focus off our storms and onto the needs of others. Your best missional-living years are ahead of you—isn't that exciting news?

Friend, we did it! We spent six weeks journeying together in God's word! I am so thankful for you. I pray you experienced refreshment and restoration in your walk with Christ. I pray you've surrendered your joy stealers and rediscovered the Jesus joy in you. Through the power of the Holy Spirit within you, walk forward in your calling as the joy-filled, missional-minded disciple you are. God desires to cultivate much fruit in and through you. Together, may we be fruit-bearing image bearers of our Creator as we walk with him in joyful and purposeful living.

Listen

Fierce Calling Podcast episode #109

Karen Kingsbury: "Making a Best-Seller Out of the Days of Your Life"

https://dorisswift.com/2022/07/12/karen-kingsbury-making-a-best-seller-out-of-the-days-of-your-life/

Fierce Calling Podcast episode #108

Mabel Ninan: "Living as Citizens of Heaven and Foreigners on Earth"

https://dorisswift.com/2022/07/05/mabel-ninan-living-as-citizens-of-heaven-and-foreigners-on-earth/

Fierce Calling Podcast episode #43

Sarah Harmeyer: "You Have a Place at Neighbor's Table"

https://dorisswift.com/2020/08/25/43-sarah-harmeyeryou-have-a-place-at-neighbors-table/

Fierce Calling Podcast episode #28

Misty Phillip: "God Wants to Spark Something New in You"

https://dorisswift.com/2020/05/12/28-god-wants-to-spark-something-new-in-you-with-guest-misty-phillip/

Fierce Calling Podcast episode #121

Charlotte Guest: "How God Confirms Our Calling and Leads Us Through the Valley"

https://dorisswift.com/2022/10/25/charlotte-guest-how-god-confirms-our-calling-and-leads-us-through-the-valley/

Fierce Calling Podcast episode #62

Deb DeArmond: "You Are Never Too Old for Adventures with God"

https://dorisswift.com/2021/07/27/62-youre-never-too-old-for-new-adventures-with-god-with-deb-dearmond-doris-swift/

LEADER'S GUIDE

Dear Leader,

Thank you for answering the call to facilitate the *Surrender the Joy Stealers* Bible study! Whether you have led studies before or are a first-time leader, I hope you'll find this guide helpful in navigating each week.

As a leader, you have an extraordinary opportunity to shepherd women and help them dig deeper into God's word. Women face unique struggles and gathering in community allows them to share, encourage one another, and to be encouraged.

When leading a study, I follow these Three Ps:

- Pray—Prayer is an essential part of our lives and leading a group is no exception. Pray every day and put on the armor of God as found in Ephesians 6:10–18. The Enemy of our souls will attempt to distract us, discourage us, and deter us from staying the course. He will try keeping group members and leaders from attending each week. Pray often for every woman in your group by name. Pray for God's direction and guidance as you study and lead. Also, remember to pray for your own soul care as you shepherd the women entrusted to you. Leaders often put the needs of others first, but a burned-out leader cannot lead with excellence as unto the Lord. You must take care of yourself. God has called you to lead and is faithful to equip you with everything you need.

- Prepare—After prayer, preparation is vital. Preparation includes diving deep into God's word, reviewing the study guide prior to group time, and perhaps, adding extra group activities. The Holy Spirit will often reveal important insights during your study time. Write them down and, if you feel led to do so, share these insights with your group. Partnering with God in preparation equips you to lead your group with confidence in Christ.
- Prioritize—You will follow a general format each week, but be flexible. Give yourself permission to change up your agenda when necessary. There's no need to fret if you don't get to every question—be sensitive to the Holy Spirit's leading during group time. Allow women to share, but be aware sharing comes with a caveat: as the leader, you must maintain control of group conversation time. Be intentional about moving the conversation along, allowing everyone an opportunity to share.

As a leader, you are shepherding women but also discipling them.

Surrender the Joy Stealers is a group study but can also be used for individual study. I highly recommend a group environment because it allows women to encourage one another.

Consider writing group members a note of encouragement when you observe spiritual growth. Group time can also provide women an opportunity to use their spiritual gifts. If a woman in your group displays leadership skills, consider asking her to lead one of the group meetings. If a woman displays the gift of encouragement, consider having her greet women at the door each week. I would also suggest inviting women in different seasons of life to join your group. I love seeing a span of generations studying the Bible together and gleaning from one another.

You are a blessing, and I am praying for you! I would love to connect with you and your group members, so reach out to me on my contact page at dorisswift.com. As a speaker, I would love the opportunity to speak at your next women's event. I am also available to pop in (virtually or in person, depending on location) during one of your group meetings as scheduling allows.

God bless you and your heart for gathering women in the word!

Much Love in Christ,

Doris

GETTING STARTED

Leading a women's Bible study is exciting kingdom work! You'll find women are eager to join Bible studies, but avoid focusing on numbers. Pray and trust God will bring the right number of women. Whether four or fourteen women sign up, God has a plan for your group. You've done your part by stepping up and being obedient to lead!

FIRST STEPS

- Decide where and when your group will meet (group time runs about one and a half to two hours). Consider possible space available in your home, in a friend's home, your church, a clubhouse, or other spaces designed for gathering
- Arrange for childcare if needed
- Provide an avenue for signups for your *Surrender the Joy Stealers* Bible study (If through your church, they might have an online form women can access. You might also consider creating an event on social media and sending invites there.)
- Ask your church, friends, and family to get the word out
- Decide if group members will purchase a copy of *Surrender the Joy Stealers* on their own, or if you will have books available for purchase at your first meeting (your church may be willing to order them for you.)
- Create a welcome letter to hand out during your first meeting. This can be a simple Word document or created on sites like canva.com. Canva is a free tool and an excellent resource for creating letters, signs, announcements, invitations, and more

YOUR WELCOME LETTER MIGHT INCLUDE:

- A personal welcome from you
- A schedule, listing session titles and dates (this is helpful if you need to skip a week)
- Expectations of group members (e.g., what is shared within the group is confidential and should not be shared elsewhere without permission, arriving on time, allowing time for everyone to share, guidelines for snacks if applicable, etc.)
- Any other pertinent details
- An encouraging message and applicable Bible verse
- Your name and contact information

SUGGESTIONS FOR YOUR FIRST GROUP SESSION

- Arrive at least thirty minutes early
- Set up a greeting table with welcome sign, name tags, markers, and sign-in sheet (your church may have an electronic check-in app you can download to track attendance)
- Have extra pens/pencils available
- Set up a table with light refreshments (This is just a suggestion. Consider having group members take turns bringing healthy snacks)
- Greet each group member as they arrive
- Begin on time and open every meeting with prayer
- Ice Breaker Introductions[1] (find great icebreaker ideas on my friend Cyndee Ownby's website: https://womensministrytoolbox.com/icebreakers-questions-for-introductions/)

At your first meeting, introduce yourself and share something interesting about you other group members might not know. Ask participants to introduce themselves and encourage them to share what drew them to this study. Have them also share an interesting fact about themselves.

Next, review How to Use This Study and what participants can expect during your six weeks together. Emphasize the importance of completing homework, but encourage participants to attend even if they have not finished all five days.

Ask group members to read the *Surrender the Joy Stealers* introduction at home prior to beginning the Week One homework.

Speaking of Week One, I want to review what was stated in the How to Use This Study section. During the first week women will identify what threatens to steal their joy. When engaging in group study, there's a caveat when it comes to relationships. *Surrender the Joy Stealers* is meant to be a journey of discovery and personal growth in Christ. If a joy stealer happens to be a spouse/friend/other family member, there is a common desire to see the other person "fixed" and experience transformation. Raw emotions may cause a woman to want to spill out every detail of her relationship issues with the group. During the first meeting, it is important for group leaders to communicate that women are encouraged to share while avoiding oversharing about someone outside the group.

In other words, we want our conversations to be seasoned with salt and honoring to the Lord. We can discuss our joy stealers without overstepping boundaries when it comes to our relationship with others. Always allow the Holy Spirit to direct the conversation, and gently redirect the flow back to how God's word provides us with solutions to experience our own transformation. The Bible helps us learn to see our lives and circumstances through a biblical lens, which changes our perspective and brings

Surrender the Joy Stealers | 179

hope and healing. The other person in a relationship may never change, but God can do a miraculous transformation in and through us, enabling us to experience his gift of joy in all circumstances.

Instruct group members to highlight and/or notate what stands out to them during each day's study time. This will help them answer discussion questions during the group gatherings.

As weeks go by, participants will get to know each other and gain a level of trust. You'll find some women eager to share, while others might need more time before feeling comfortable doing so. Allow women to share as they feel led. It's remarkable what women glean from God and each other in an environment where they feel safe to share thoughts and experiences.

You will learn to discern when to spend more time on a question and when to move on. Participants will appreciate your commitment to begin and end each week's session on time.

Use the remainder of the first group session time for Q & A, refreshments, and optional prayer requests. You as the leader will decide how to handle prayer requests within your group. You can schedule time to pray for requests during the group meeting, ask the women to pray for needs during the week, or opt to keep prayer focused on the study.

Week One: Reveal

Open with prayer.
Read Psalm 91
Discussion Questions:
1. What did God reveal to you during your study time on this week?
2. Which study day had the most impact on you?

3. What new insights about God were revealed to you this week?
4. What new insights about yourself were revealed to you this week?
5. Did anything surprise you during your study time?

Close in prayer (specifically pray for Week Two—Respond. Group members surrender their joy stealers and prayer is essential in letting them go).

Week Two—Respond

Open with prayer.
Read Psalm 46
Discussion Questions:
1. What did God reveal to you during your study time this week?
2. Which study day had the most impact on you?
3. What new insights about God were revealed to you this week?
4. What new insights about yourself were revealed to you this week?
5. What did you experience after surrendering your joy stealers to God?

Close in prayer.

Week Three—Receive

Open with prayer.
Read John 15:1–8
Discussion Questions:
1. What did God reveal to you during your study time this week?
2. Which study day had the most impact on you?
3. What new insights about God were revealed to you this week?
4. What new insights about yourself were revealed to you this week?

5. Did you gain a new perspective on what it means to receive?

Close in prayer.

Week Four—Renew

Open with prayer
Read Isaiah 40:31
Discussion Questions:
1. What did God reveal to you during your study time this week?
2. Which study day had the most impact on you?
3. What new insights about God were revealed to you this week?
4. What new insights about yourself were revealed to you this week?
5. Prior to the meeting, print or write out the definitions of "renew" and "awake" or access a dictionary via cellphone during the meeting.

Then ask:
6. What connections do you see between renew and awake?

Close in prayer.

Week Five—Rest

Open with prayer.
Read Matthew 11:29
Discussion Questions:
1. What did God reveal to you during your study time this week?
2. Which study day had the most impact on you?
3. What new insights about God were revealed to you this week?
4. What new insights about yourself were revealed to you this week?

5. What new insights about rest were revealed to you this week?

Close in prayer.

Week Six—Reach

Open with prayer.
Read John 15:26–27
Discussion Questions:
1. How can we live missionally in our homes?
2. How can we live missionally in our churches?
3. How can we live missionally in our communities?
4. What is your Missional Living Plan?

OPTIONAL ACTIVITY

Brainstorm missional living ideas with your group. Missional living goes beyond a one-time service project, it's about building relationships.

Here are a few ideas on building relationships.

- Prayer is always the priority—pray for God to open your eyes to divine appointments and the ones he is calling you to connect with and serve
- Children's home or foster care community. Ask how your group can serve well and be part of their mission
- Women's shelters
- Schools
- Faith-based pregnancy centers
- Hot meal programs
- Cultivate missional groups within homes where neighbors are invited in, friends can bring friends, and get to know one another over meals and conversations

Those are just a few ideas, and we can learn to be

intentional while allowing the Lord to lead. Building relationships is not about an agenda or checking off a spiritual to-do box, but about reaching people with the hope we have in Christ. As we allow others into our lives, they'll witness how we do life with Jesus.

Divine encounters happen every day, but if we're not careful, we might miss them. There are also those brief encounter divine appointments—times when God purposefully sits you next to someone on a plane or positions you behind a hurting woman at the grocery store. Those encounters can make an impact too, and as we covered in Week Six, 1 Peter 3:15 tells us we must always be ready to give an answer when asked about the hope we have. We are all called to share the good news.

Isn't it amazing how our callings are interwoven into our everyday lives. As Jesus said in John 15:5, apart from him we can do nothing. God didn't create us for nothing and to do nothing, and he will always provide something he is calling us to do. Listen for his voice and when we love like Jesus, we are impacting the world in ways far beyond ourselves. We are all part of God's big-picture plan! When we surrender our joy stealers and move forward in our call to missional living, we are partnering with God and others in furthering his kingdom. You are chosen and called, equipped and empowered, and best of all, loved with an everlasting love. Walk boldly in your calling and fully experience the Jesus joy in you.

BONUS SECTION: SIMPLE TIPS FOR SHARING YOUR FAITH

Do you ever get tongue-tied sharing the gospel with others? I used to put so much pressure on myself, wanting to say the perfect words so others would accept Jesus. Isn't it a relief that saving people is not our job? God is the one who transforms hearts, but he uses us to share the good news.

I want to help you share your faith with the people God places in your path. I've created a helpful resource called "Simple Tips for Sharing Your Faith" just for you. This resource is a free downloadable pdf with tips about sharing your grace story and a full page of applicable Bible verses. You can find the tips at https://dorisswift.com/shareyourfaith. Jesus placed eternity in us so we could tell others about him. May the Lord our God bless you as you partner with him in kingdom work.

ABOUT THE AUTHOR

Doris Swift is an author, speaker, founder of Fierce Calling Ministries, and podcast host of the award-winning Fierce Calling Podcast. In ministry for more than thirty years, Doris is passionate about encouraging and equipping women to walk deeper in God's word, take action where their passion, compassion, and conviction intersect, and use their God-given gifts to impact the world for Christ. Doris's writing has been featured on popular sites such as "(in)courage," *Just Between Us* magazine, "Life Letter Café," "Thrive Global," "Purposeful Faith," and "Arise Daily." She has had numerous articles published in Medium's *The Ascent, Publishous*, and *Startups and Venture Capital*.

Doris self-published *Goodbye-Regret: Forgiving Yourself of Past Mistakes* in 2016, and contributed a chapter to the award-winning book compilation *We May Be Done But We're Not Finished* by author Deb DeArmond, published by Elk Lake Publishing, Inc., in 2021. She has been interviewed on several radio shows and podcasts, featured in the author spotlight on *Publishous*, and sold one of her popular quotes to DaySpring for their product line.

Doris has served as Women's Ministry Director at her church and enjoys speaking at women's events both in-person and virtually. As a lay counselor and discipleship mentor, she counsels women during the most difficult seasons of their lives. She holds a Bachelor of Science in Interdisciplinary Studies from Liberty University in Christian counseling, psychology, and business.

Doris currently resides in Florida with her awesomely supportive husband, Brian, and their curious cat named Oliver (Liv for short). She loves Jesus, gathering around the table with family and friends, and spending time with their children and grandchildren. She also loves reading good books and sipping fancy caramel coffee with whipped cream.

ENDNOTES

Week One
1. A. W. Tozer, *The Pursuit of God* (Camp Hill: Christian Publications, Inc., 1993), 31

Week Two
1. *Merriam-Webster.com Dictionary*, s.v. "surrender," accessed June 12, 2022, https://www.merriam-webster.com/dictionary/surrender.
2. Elisabeth Ginsburg, "How Do Flowers Become Fruit?", *SFGate* https://homeguides.sfgate.com/flowers-become-fruit-58733.html

Week Three
1. D. A. Carson, *The Gospel according to John, The Pillar New Testament Commentary* (Leicester: Wm. B. Eerdmans, 1991), 518.
2. James Strong, *Strong's Exhaustive Concordance of the Bible*: (Peabody, MA. Hendrickson Publishers, 2009).

Week Four
1. Dennis Durst, "Soul," ed. John D. Barry et al., *The Lexicon Bible Dictionary* (Bellingham, WA: Lexham Press, 2016), accessed from Logos Bible software 10/01/2022.
2. Joel T. Hamme, "Soul," ed. Douglas Mangum et al., *Lexham Theological Wordbook*, Lexham Bible Reference Series (Bellingham, WA: Lexham Press, 2014), accessed from Logos Bible software 10/01/2022.

3. J. I. Packer, *Knowing God* (Downers Grove, IL: InterVarsity Press, 1973) 34.
4. Francis Chan, *Forgotten God: Reversing Our Tragic Neglect of the Holy Spirit* (Colorado Springs: David C Cook 2009), 25.
5. Caroline Leaf, *Switch on Your Brain: The Key to Peak Happiness, Thinking, and Health.* (Grand Rapids: Baker, 2013).

Week Six
1. Mabel Ninan, *Far from Home: Discovering Your Identity as Foreigners on Earth.* (Birmingham, AL: Harambee Press, 2022).

Leader's Guide
1. "31 Great Icebreaker Questions for Introductions," Women's Ministry Toolbox, January 16, 2018, https://womensministrytoolbox.com/icebreaker-questions-for-introductions/.